FROM

PALM

SUNDAY

TO

EASTER

SUNDAY

"*From Palm Sunday to Easter Sunday* is a perfect read during the Easter season or any time of the year for readers eager to learn about the events surrounding the greatest miracle in our world's history: the Atonement of Jesus Christ. Using Brother Christiansen's day-by-day recap of the final eight days of Jesus's life, readers can not only learn the details about what led to His triumph over death but also walk away with relevant personal application in the Questions to Ponder section at the end of each chapter. While more than two billion human beings believe in Christ as the resurrected Son of God, the doctrines and principles of application provided by Brother Christiansen add a world of insights about Jesus's role as Savior, Redeemer, and King and about our role as His disciples. This is a perfect book to help strengthen testimony of why these final days changed the world—and our lives—forever."

—Eric D. Richards, beloved speaker and author of *Great Mess to Greatness* and *Preparing for the Second Coming*

"In *From Palm Sunday to Easter Sunday*, Brother Christiansen provides a thoughtful review of the last days of the Savior's mortal ministry. He clearly has a love for the Lord and a good understanding of the meaningful doctrines the Master taught. Each chapter concludes with excellent thought-provoking questions that will help readers increase faith and strengthen testimony. This book is an excellent volume for those who desire to learn more about the final week of the Savior's life and develop a better understanding of the gospel of Jesus Christ."

—David T. Morgan, PhD, author of *My God Hath Been My Support*

FROM PALM SUNDAY TO EASTER SUNDAY

Journey with Christ through His Final Days

STEPHEN R. CHRISTIANSEN

Covenant Communications, Inc.

Cover image *Jesus Christ Extending Welcoming Hand* © Ryan J. Lane, istockphoto.com

Cover design by Christina Marcano © 2019 by Covenant Communications, Inc.

Published by Covenant Communications, Inc.
American Fork, Utah

Copyright © 2019 by Stephen R. Christiansen
All rights reserved. No part of this book may be reproduced in any format or in any medium without the written permission of the publisher, Covenant Communications, Inc., P.O. Box 416, American Fork, UT 84003. This work is not an official publication of The Church of Jesus Christ of Latter-day Saints. The views expressed within this work are the sole responsibility of the author and do not necessarily reflect the position of The Church of Jesus Christ of Latter-day Saints, Covenant Communications, Inc., or any other entity.

This material is neither made, provided, approved, nor endorsed by Intellectual Reserve, Inc. or The Church of Jesus Christ of Latter-day Saints. Any content or opinions expressed, implied or included in or with the material are solely those of the owner and not those of Intellectual Reserve, Inc. or The Church of Jesus Christ of Latter-day Saints.

Printed in the United States of America
First Printing: March 2019

25 24 23 22 21 20 19   10 9 8 7 6 5 4 3 2 1

ISBN 978-1-52440-874-9

For Suzanne,
Always selfless, striving, and supportive

Table of Contents

Preface..vii

Introduction..1

Day One: Palm Sunday..5

Day Two: Monday..17

Day Three: Tuesday...29

Day Four: Wednesday..45

Day Five: Thursday..51

Day Six: Friday..65

Day Seven: Saturday..81

Day Eight: Easter Sunday..93

Epilogue..105

Bibliography..111

Preface

On Palm Sunday, April 9, 2017, my wife and I sat in the general session of our stake conference. As the meeting progressed, I began to appreciate how Christ-centered this meeting was and the resulting Spirit that was present. Suddenly a prompting came, clear and unmistakable, for me to send an email every day that week to my family, summarizing the events of each day in the final week of Christ's life, from His last Sunday as a mortal being, known today as Palm Sunday, to Easter, or Resurrection Sunday. In addition, the Spirit instructed me to share with my family some of my own insights, feelings, testimony, and love for my Savior.

Each day I would study multiple sources, including the scriptures, Elder James E. Talmage's *Jesus the Christ*, W. Jeffrey Marsh's *His Final Hours*, Elder Bruce R. McConkie's *The Mortal Messiah* series, and other wonderful resources. This focused endeavor consumed me. Of course, I could not simply push the pause button on the rest of my life; work and other normal activities continued. Therefore, I awoke early and studied during every available moment I could—while riding public transportation to and from work, during lunch, and so forth. Then, after enjoying dinner with my wife, I would spend two to four hours writing before clicking the Send button. Each morning I would awake and begin again, studying the events of the next day of Christ's life during what has become known in the Christian world as Holy Week.

When Easter Sunday, April 16, 2017, arrived, the spirit of the sacrament hymn seemed to wash over me like a warm ocean wave. I found that the words to that hymn and to the sacrament prayers came with greater intensity and meaning than usual.

I was scheduled to teach Gospel Doctrine that Sunday. The lesson I had prepared seemed so insignificant when compared with the impression that I should speak and testify of Christ, so that is what I did. For forty minutes I recounted from memory a summary of the emails I had sent my family the previous week and bore solemn testimony of the Savior. The Spirit filled the room, not because of me but because "we talk[ed] of Christ, we rejoice[d] in Christ, we preach[ed] of Christ, we prophes[ied] of Christ . . ." (2 Nephi 25:26).

When I had sent the last email to my family, I was physically exhausted but spiritually aflame. Over the course of the next few weeks, I compiled the emails into a single document and shared it privately with a few people. Their reaction was much the same as what had occurred in Gospel Doctrine that Easter Sunday. As I reflected on the sweetness of this experience, I felt that perhaps sharing the content more formally with others would represent, in part, a simple way to testify of Christ and help others come unto and be blessed by Him.

I invite you to make this book yours. Read it, write in it, digest it, and thoughtfully answer the questions at the end of each chapter, which encourage pondering and thoughtful introspection. If the benefit you derive is significant, and I hope it will be, consider making the reading of this book an annual tradition, studying one chapter per day, from Palm Sunday to Easter Sunday.

Elder Dieter F. Uchtdorf said, "It is fitting that during the week from Palm Sunday to Easter morning we turn our thoughts to Jesus Christ, the source of light, life, and love."[1] It is also notable that in latter days, the Lord has chosen to celebrate Holy Week in unique ways. For example, it was on Palm Sunday in 1836 that the Kirtland Temple was dedicated and attended to by a glorious heavenly host. During the Holy Week that followed, events of great significance and spiritual import occurred. Then, culminating on Easter Sunday, April 3, 1836, Jesus Christ appeared to His prophet in His House. I have found that the Lord is very often chronologically consistent when choosing dates for important events in the history of this world.

I intentionally tried to keep this book relatively short, making, for the reader, the establishment of an annual tradition easier. In doing so, choosing what to exclude from the record was just as difficult as choosing what to include. There are multiple comprehensive resources describing Christ's life, written in great detail, prolifically expounding His life and teachings. However, I knew that if this book

---

[1] Dieter F. Uchtdorf, "The Way of the Disciple," *Ensign* or *Liahona*, May 2009, 75.

were to accomplish its objective, it needed to be long enough to capture the substance and deep emotion of the events of the Savior's last few days of mortality while being short enough to be consumable by all in reasonable daily portions that would hopefully culminate in a powerful one-week experience.

The sequence of events during Christ's final week varies somewhat significantly by Gospel writer. While I have attempted to accurately attribute each event to the correct day of that week, doing so precisely was impossible, given historical inconsistencies, and, frankly, was not my primary objective. My principal motivation was to create a resource that is an accurate reflection of the substance of those final days and, importantly, captures the spirit and emotion of those gut-wrenching and awe-inspiring occurrences. I have also included lyrics from sacred hymns toward the end of each chapter to help accentuate the experience.

The purpose of life is to become one with Jesus Christ as we learn of Him, seek to become like Him, and increasingly feel His love and power in our lives. If you approach this book with a humble heart and a desire to feel His perfect love, I promise it will come. I promise you will feel an increased closeness to Him.

As you seek to more fully understand what Jesus experienced firsthand, you likely will feel a range of emotions. These emotions may run the gamut, as did mine, from joy and happiness to peace and wonder to moments of sorrow, grief, and sadness, culminating on Easter Sunday with renewed feelings of joy and exultation. But, more than anything, I pray you will feel love—deep, abiding love—for Christ, who was

From Palm Sunday to Easter Sunday

completely obedient to His Father's will and who proclaimed His own divine Sonship; paid the predetermined, dreadful price; and, in the end, came off victorious. It is inspiring to know that because He was victorious over sin and death, so can we be, through Him. As you conclude this Preface, consider the words to the first verse of the hymn "I Stand all Amazed."

> I stand all amazed at the love Jesus offers me,
> Confused at the grace that so fully He proffers me.
> I tremble to know that for me He was crucified,
> That for me, a sinner, he suffered, he bled and died.
>
> Oh, it is wonderful
> That he should care for me
> Enough to die for me!
> Oh, it is wonderful,
> Wonderful to me![2]

---

2 "I Stand All Amazed," *Hymns*, no. 193.

Introduction

THERE WAS SOMETHING MORE THAN special about this man called Jesus of Nazareth. His detractors could not confound Him. His disciples could not fully appreciate Him. His closest friends could not bear to leave Him. The magnitude of His mission and sacrifice was not fully understood during His mortal life, nor is it even now. The culmination of the last few days of His mortality in His Atonement and Resurrection would forever testify of Him, not as a great moral teacher but as the very Son of God and Savior of the world. Those events would forever remove all doubt of His real identity. C. S. Lewis justifiably argued the point:

> I am trying here to prevent anyone saying the really foolish thing that people often say about Him: 'I'm ready to accept Jesus as a great moral teacher, but I don't accept His claim to be God.' That is the one thing we must not say. A man who was merely a man and said the sort of things Jesus said [and did

all that Jesus did] would not be a great moral teacher. He would either be a lunatic . . . or else he would be the Devil of Hell. You must make your choice. Either this man was, and is, the Son of God: or else a madman or something worse. You can shut Him up for a fool, you can spit at Him and kill Him as a demon; or you can fall at His feet and call Him Lord and God. But let us not come with any patronising nonsense about His being a great human teacher. He has not left that open to us.[3]

Christ's final days began and ended triumphantly, but what occurred in between must have often felt to Him nothing of the sort. Jesus rode an unassuming donkey into Jerusalem amidst the swelling throng of passionate disciples who thought He had come to conquer Roman rule, yet did not realize His kingdom was "not of this world" (John 18:36). In a spirit of righteous indignation, Jesus cleansed the temple a second time during His mortal ministry in respect for His Father's house and to restore a spirit of peace and reverence to that once-sacred precinct. Jesus vigorously censured the scribes and Pharisees, calling them hypocrites. He taught parables and offered His final public prayer, the incomparable great Intercessory Prayer, and instituted new ordinances, one of which is designed to help us "always remember him" (D&C 20:77) and the suffering He willingly and unimaginably endured for every

---

3 C. S. Lewis, *Mere Christianity*, in *The Complete C. S. Lewis Signature Classics* (New York City: HarperCollins, 2002), 36.

sin and affliction inherent in this mortal condition. In His weakened state, Jesus was unlawfully tried at the hands of a hate-filled, jealous mob and condemned to death. The crime? Blasphemy—inconceivably, the very Jehovah allegedly blasphemed Jehovah. Jesus was scourged, mocked, and spit upon. Bloodied and beaten, He was cruelly nailed to a cross. While hanging in agony, Jesus *again* suffered for the sins, pains, and afflictions of all mankind, and that time He did it completely alone. Jesus's body was laid in a borrowed tomb while He preached the everlasting gospel to the long-awaiting spirits in paradise. But the ultimate triumph is that, on the third day, He arose!

Such are some of the experiences that occurred during that week of weeks. From the beginning of time, no combined events over the course of a single week can compare to those that transpired during that first Holy Week in Jesus's life. In essence, everything Christ did seemed focused on fulfilling ancient prophecy, testifying of His divinity, boldly declaring the apostasy that had crept into Judaism and its leaders, lovingly preparing His faithful followers for what lay ahead, and perfectly fulfilling the will of His Father.

Jesus was foreordained before the creation of this world to atone for all of God's creations (D&C 76:40–42).[4] His mortal ministry lasted only three years. He taught eternally life-changing doctrine, wrought awe-inspiring miracles, and performed sacred ordinances. His primary mission was to atone, and so He pressed forward, knowing His time was short and the indescribably agonizing requirements that lay before Him had to be satisfied.

---

4 Tad R. Callister, *The Infinite Atonement* (Salt Lake City: Deseret Book, 2000), 83–90.

Indeed, the events of His last week on Earth would add infinite purpose to the eternal existence of every man, woman, and child who would accept Him as Savior and Redeemer.

Day One
PALM SUNDAY

CHAPTER PREVIEW

As with most days that week, Palm Sunday began with Jesus and His Apostles making the two-mile trek from Bethany, home to some of His most beloved friends, to Jerusalem. Along the way, Christ sent two of His Apostles to nearby Bethphage to obtain conveyance in the form of a donkey. The donkey was sought, not because the journey was long and arduous but because there was prophecy to be fulfilled. In fulfillment of that ancient prophesy, Christ mounted the donkey and rode triumphantly through the eastern gate into Jerusalem, hailed by the Jews as the great Emancipator who would come to free Israel from the bondage of Roman rule. On this day His people openly acknowledged His divine Sonship, and He permitted it. Ironically, later in the week, with equal intensity, some of the same people would demand His execution.

THE FINAL SUNDAY OF CHRIST'S mortal life occurred on what has since become known as Palm Sunday and was in close proximity to the eight-day Jewish Passover, or Feast of Unleavened Bread, celebration. Most of the final days of Christ's life in mortality were spent in Jerusalem. The evenings were spent in a nearby town called Bethany. Here lived three of his most-beloved disciples and friends. First, of course, was Mary, whom Elder Bruce R. McConkie described thus: "And in the souls of none did the fires of love, and devotion, and worship, burn more brightly than in the soul of the beloved Mary. She who loved to sit at Jesus' feet and hear his words; she whose soul drank in truth as the parched desert absorbs the heaven-sent rain."[5] Such devotion to the Master has none other demonstrated as Mary; who, days later, would see Jesus crucified, His body laid in a borrowed tomb; and then be the first to witness the risen Lord. Next was her sister, Martha, the "careful and troubled" (Luke 10:41) one who had previously been taught by her Lord the difference between "good, better, and best."[6] The third was their cherished brother, Lazarus, whom Jesus loved and had miraculously risen from the dead. As Elder McConkie described, "we must note the intimate and felicitous friendships that prevailed between Jesus and the beloved sisters and their brother Lazarus. We have reason to believe this relationship was like none other enjoyed by him."[7] Christ spent the evenings during His final days on Earth with these cherished friends and with His beloved associates, the Apostles, and likely others.

Most days during His final week on Earth, Jesus would walk from Bethany to Jerusalem, nearly two miles to the west. The course took Him over the Mount of Olives, descended

---

[5] Bruce R. McConkie, *The Mortal Messiah: From Bethlehem to Calvary*, vol. 3, (Salt Lake City: Deseret Book, 1980), 335.

[6] Dallin H. Oaks, "Good, Better, Best," *Ensign* or *Liahona*, Nov. 2007, 104.

[7] Bruce R. McConkie, *The Mortal Messiah: From Bethlehem to Calvary*, vol. 3, (Salt Lake City: Deseret Book, 1980), 333.

From Palm Sunday to Easter Sunday

into the Kidron Valley, and then climbed up into the city through the eastern, or Golden, gate to the temple, where He would preach on several occasions. The symbolism of that journey must have caused moments of contemplation as He anticipated the events that awaited Him. Think of the imagery, as captured by W. Jeffrey Marsh: "This walk foreshadowed the spiritual path he would tread in his final hours. It was a prefiguring of his descent through Gethsemane's agony down into death and the spirit world and then back up again into the presence of the Father."[8]

Since Christ's raising of Lazarus not many days before, the Jewish leaders had been conspiring to capture Jesus and put Him to death in order to quell the growing fervor for our Lord's presence and works. Despite this real and imminent threat, Jesus knew His mission was not yet complete and His life would only be taken when He allowed it to happen. Elder McConkie spoke of this fact, paraphrasing John 11:9–10 as follows:

> Certainly Jesus would go to Judea in spite of the threats of death that faced him there. "Though it be the eleventh hour of my life, yet there are twelve hours in the day, and during that designated period, I shall do the work appointed me without stumbling or faltering. This is the time given me to do my work. I cannot wait for the night when perchance the opposition will die down. He that shirks his responsibilities and puts off

---

[8] W. Jeffrey Marsh, *His Final Hours* (Salt Lake City: Deseret Book, 2000), 21.

his labors until the night shall stumble in the darkness and fail in his work."[9]

So He proceeded. Jesus knew full well the events that awaited Him in Jerusalem during the last week of His life. He could have turned and fled, never to return to the holy city. However, such was never His attitude. He had always been, and would always be, committed to fulfilling His Father's will and doing *all* things necessary to bless you and me.

On that first Palm Sunday, after He had departed Bethany and summited the Mount of Olives, Jesus, demonstrating the gift of seership, sent two of his disciples to nearby Bethphage, saying unto them, "Go into the village over against you, and straightway ye shall find an ass tied, and a colt with her: loose them, and bring them unto me. And if any man say ought unto you, ye shall say, The Lord hath need of them; and straightway he will send them" (Matthew 21:2–3). It was on this donkey that Jesus intended to enter the city of Jerusalem that day.

Many, especially Matthew, who paid particular attention in his record to all things that fulfilled ancient prophecy, believe the Savior's entrance was in fulfillment of the words of Zechariah, which say, "behold, thy King cometh unto thee: he is just, and having salvation; lowly, and riding upon an ass" (Zechariah 9:9). What a perfect description of our Savior Jesus Christ in many regards, including those expounded upon below:

"Thy King"

As Elder James E. Talmage has explained, "Had Judah been a free and independent nation, ruled by

---

[9] Bruce R. McConkie, *Doctrinal New Testament Commentary: The Gospels*, vol. 1, (Salt Lake City: Bookcraft, Inc., 1976), 531.

her rightful sovereign, Joseph the carpenter would have been her crowned king; and his lawful successor to the throne would have been Jesus of Nazareth, the King of the Jews."[10] Indeed, though Jesus was every bit a king in an eternal perspective, He also would have been reigning over the house of Israel in Jerusalem had the Romans not conquered about a hundred years before.

"He is just"

No one is more just or merciful than Jesus Christ. As Nephi declared, "O the greatness and the justice of our God! For he executeth all his words, and they have gone forth out of his mouth, and his law must be fulfilled" (2 Nephi 9:17).

"Having salvation"

Jesus became the central figure in the Father's Plan of Salvation from the moment in the pre-mortal world when His selfless offering, "send me" (Abraham 3:27), was accepted. On that triumphant day in Jerusalem, and forever, Jesus came offering to all the hope and promise of immortality and the eternal possibility of exaltation. Furthermore, through the enabling power of His Atonement, He can "succor the weak, lift up the hands which hang down, and strengthen the feeble knees" (D&C 81:5).

"Lowly"

Is it not Jesus, the greatest of all, who is servant of all and was born in a lowly stable? Is it not Jesus who said, "Foxes have holes, and birds of the air have nests; but the

---

10 James E. Talmage, *Jesus the Christ* (Salt Lake City: Deseret Book Company, 1982), 87.

Son of man hath not where to lay his head" (Luke 9:58)? Finally, is it not Jesus who demonstrated perfectly His own counsel when He taught His Apostles, "If any man desire to be first, the same shall be last of all, and servant of all" (Mark 9:35)? Without question, Jesus perfectly epitomizes the adjective *lowly*.

"Riding upon an ass"

Anciently, kings who intended to conquer came riding upon a horse, a symbol of war. However, Jesus, King of the Jews and Prince of Peace, came "riding upon an ass" (Zechariah 9:9). A donkey is an ancient symbol of Jewish royalty and of peaceful progress. This reference also highlights Matthew's frequent portrayal of our Savior as the Son of David.[11]

As Christ mounted the donkey and entered Jerusalem through the eastern gate, located where the Golden Gate now stands, He was thronged with people on all sides. Some had gathered and come with Him from Bethany, while others joined in the celebration in Jerusalem. At that moment, many viewed Him as their literal king, though only five days later He would hang on the cross, rejected, alone. Many believed Him to be the foretold Messiah who would come to liberate them from the shackles of Roman rule and usher in a period of peace and prosperity. Some certainly noticed the symbolism of His entry and assumed the long-awaited day had arrived. It is likely others were simply caught up in the excitement of the occasion. They threw down palm branches

---

11 Eric D. Huntsman, *God So Loved the World: The Final Days of the Savior's Life* (Salt Lake City: Deseret Book, 2001), 11.

along His path and exclaimed the Hosanna Shout, both actions symbols of the Feast of Tabernacles and indicative of their joyous recognition of Jehovah as the King of Israel.

Elder Bruce R. McConkie commented on the scene as follows:

> No other man ever lived to whom such inspired acclamations of adulation, reverence, and worship have been or could properly be made. Here we see great multitudes bearing testimony of our Lord's divine Sonship. In plain language they are hailing Jesus as the Son of David, the Deliverer of Israel, their Savior and Redeemer, the promised Messiah, the Son of God. And they are doing it wittingly, deliberately using the sacred expression, *Hosanna*, and quoting from the Messianic prophecy which ascribes salvation and triumph to the promised Son of David.[12]

It is the Apostle John who provides partial explanation as to the crowd's willingness to accept Christ as the possible Messiah (John 12:17–18). Not many days before, Christ had raised Lazarus from the dead. Though it was not the first such exercise of priesthood power, it seemed to have cemented in the minds of the people Christ's potential role as Deliverer of the Jewish nation. Elder Dieter F. Uchtdorf captures the hopeful expectation that "perhaps [even] the disciples thought this was a turning point—the moment when the Jewish world

---

[12] Bruce R. McConkie, *Doctrinal New Testament Commentary: The Gospels*, vol. 1, (Salt Lake City: Bookcraft, Inc., 1976), 578–79.

would finally recognize Jesus as the long-awaited Messiah. But the Savior understood that many of the shouts of praise and acclamation would be temporary. He knew that soon He would ascend to the Mount of Olives and there, alone in Gethsemane, take upon Himself the sins of the world."[13] It seemed that everyone except the Jewish leaders, whose craft was threatened by this man called Jesus, hoped that He who came "riding upon an ass" was the long-awaited Emancipator. While the people in general rejoiced at His coming, imagine the self-righteous Jewish leaders beholding the treatment this Man of Galilee was receiving and the jealousy, ire, and anger that continued to swell in their hearts.

A pause may be appropriate to point out additional symbolism. Note Jesus's glorious arrival and majestic entrance into Jerusalem. As mentioned earlier, some who welcomed Him had come with Him from Bethany, while others He encountered in Jerusalem. In a future day, not many years hence, Jesus again will come in glorious majesty. On that occasion He will bring with Him the resurrected righteous and will encounter on the earth the righteous who have been spared the destruction of the wicked. Together they will celebrate His arrival and eternal reign as "King of kings, and Lord of lords" (1 Timothy 6:15). Unlike His first and triumphant arrival into Jerusalem, during which the majority of those who received Him eventually turned against Him, at His Second Coming those who receive Him will recognize Him, accept Him, and gladly submit to His eternal reign.

During that first triumphal entry, with the crowd boisterous, the Pharisees, filled with an opposing spirit, approached

---

13 Dieter F. Uchtdorf, "The Way of the Disciple," *Ensign* or *Liahona*, May 2009, 75.

From Palm Sunday to Easter Sunday

Jesus and commanded that He rebuke His disciples. Jesus's reply was most interesting. "If these should hold their peace, the stones would immediately cry out" (Luke 19:40), He said, suggesting that even if the throngs were to be silenced, the very rocks He had created ages before and which knew precisely who He is, would cry out, worshiping Him. Early in His ministry Jesus went to great lengths to avoid announcing that He was indeed the promised Messiah. Now, His mortal mission was coming to an end, and this would be one of several occasions during His last mortal week when He would permit and even personally declare His divine Sonship.

At some point during Palm Sunday, Jesus's feelings became weighed down, perhaps as He viewed the hypocritical Jewish leaders who were committed to finding a way to take His life or perhaps as He anticipated His impending sacrifice. With such heavy feelings, He prayed, "Father, glorify thy name." In response "came there a voice from heaven saying, I have both glorified it, and will glorify it again" (John 12:28). Many standing around heard the noise. Some thought it was thunder. Others thought it was an angel speaking to Christ. Perhaps others, but probably few, correctly understood the source.

Now, perhaps feeling a spirit of invigoration, Jesus proclaimed, as if the triumph of His Atonement had already taken place, "Now is the judgment of this world: now shall the prince of this world be cast out" (John 12:31). Satan, the "prince of this world," knows he is doomed, but he will fight to the end, seeking always to oppose that which is good, and, specifically that week, to prevent the prophesied Redemption from occurring. These two participants in the premortal council of heaven, who offered themselves to come to Earth and atone, were now practically face-to-face, and the singular pivotal moment in the history of the world would soon transpire. Which of these two, the Firstborn or Perdition, would prevail?

From the moment in the premortal existence when Satan's self-aggrandizing offer was rejected, his motivation to destroy everything that is good and righteous and leads to God became fixed. Throughout the history of the world, Satan has been present at critical junctures and throughout has sought to thwart his Father's plan. He was there in the Garden of Eden, tempting Eve to partake. He reigned seemingly triumphant in the days of Noah when the world, save eight, lived in wickedness. At the beginning of Christ's mortal ministry, he tempted Jesus, seeking to cause Him to serve Himself rather than those He had come to save. On that first Palm Sunday, Satan reigned in the hearts of the Jewish leaders who would, not many days hence, secure permission from Pilate to have their own Jehovah crucified. The adversary was present and unleashed his fury later in that final week as Christ suffered willingly and unimaginably in the Garden and on the cross. He prompted the killing of Christ's Apostles during the few decades that followed Jesus's own martyrdom. He reigned seemingly supreme during the centuries of darkness that preceded the latter-day Restoration. Knowing the light that was about to burst forth upon the earth and the saving ordinances, covenants, and gospel that were about to be restored, Satan was present in the Sacred Grove when Joseph prayed to the Father. Nearly thirty-nine years later, he was present to motivate the killing of the prophet of the dispensation of the fulness of times in Carthage Jail. And he has been present at so many other times throughout the history of the world, seeking

From Palm Sunday to Easter Sunday 15

always to thwart and destroy; while the Father, through the Son, continually seeks to lift, edify, succor, and save. Toward the end of that first Palm Sunday, Jesus gave hope when He said, "And I, if I be lifted up from the earth, will draw all men unto me" (John 12:32).

Despite the opposition, Jesus had nearly completed this first day of His final week of mortality. The first and triumphant Palm Sunday was drawing to a close. Jesus had allowed the throngs to rightfully acknowledge Him as King. He had overcome the threats of the hate-filled Jewish priests. Now, I invite you to reflect on the words of the hymn "All Glory, Laud, and Honor" that summarize so fittingly this eventful day.

> All glory, laud, and honor
> To Thee, Redeemer, King,
> To whom the lips of children
> Made sweet hosannas ring.
> Thou art the King of Israel,
> Thou David's royal Son,
> Who in the Lord's name comest,
> The King and Blessed One.
>
> The company of angels
> Are praising Thee on high,
> And mortal men and all things
> Created make reply.
> The people of the Hebrews
> With palms before Thee went;
> Our praise and love and anthems
> Before Thee we present.

> To Thee, before thy passion,
> They sang their hymns of praise;
> To Thee, now high exalted,
> Our melody we raise.
> Thou didst accept their praises;
> Accept the love we bring,
> Who in all good delightest,
> Thou good and gracious King.[14]

Questions to Ponder

- On several occasions during His final week as He journeyed from Bethany to Jerusalem, Jesus descended through Gethsemane, where He would ultimately come nigh unto death. He then ascended to the temple, prefiguring His glorious and eternal reunion with His Father. What do you feel as you contemplate the events that awaited Him?
- Few of the Jews recognized Jesus, not as a physical liberator from bondage to the Romans but as the promised Messiah who would free them from the yoke of sin and provide the opportunity for eternal life. How do you recognize Him?
- Few times during His mortal ministry did our Savior openly announce His divine Sonship. Palm Sunday was one of those obvious exceptions. Someday, a much larger gathering will welcome Him again, perhaps uttering the same Hosannas and acknowledging Him as the spiritual liberator He truly is. Contemplating that glorious future day, what might you feel as you witness His coming and greet Him as "King of Kings, and Lord of Lords" (Revelation 19:16)?

---

14 "All Glory, Laud, and Honor," *Hymns*, no. 69.

Day Two
MONDAY

CHAPTER PREVIEW

Monday began with Christ demonstrating His power to smite and destroy—in this case, a barren fig tree. With such demonstration, He figuratively warned everyone of the danger of hypocrisy. Later, many who were blind and lame benefited from His love and healing power. Children, whose spirits were in tune with the Spirit and who recognized Christ for who He really is, proclaimed "Hosanna to the Son of David" (Matthew 21:15), while angry priests, filled with a vile spirit, denounced such adulations. But perhaps the most significant of the day's events occurred as He, for a second time during His mortal ministry, forcefully cleansed the temple of the temporal and spiritual filth that had occupied that sacred precinct. In doing so, He reminded everyone of the importance of reverence for sacred things and places and of His promise that if we "do not suffer any unclean thing to come into [the House of the Lord], that it be not defiled, [His] glory shall rest upon it" (D&C 97:15).

JESUS AND THE TWELVE BEGAN the journey early Monday from Bethany to Jerusalem, where He would spend the better part of the day in the temple. Along the way the group approached a fig tree that looked different than others usually did that early in the season. Normally the fruit buds of the tree would be in bloom, followed thereafter by the leaves and fruit. However, this tree was already full of leaves. As they drew near, it became apparent that leaves were all it bore—Elder Talmage explained that it was nothing more than a "showy, fruitless, barren tree"—whereupon the Savior pronounced "the sentence of perpetual barrenness" by saying, "No man eat fruit of thee hereafter for ever" (Mark 11:14).[15] Shortly thereafter the fig tree withered and died.

Pronouncing such a harsh sentence may seem unjustified, but there were likely at least three reasons for doing so. First, the Savior had fully demonstrated His power to heal and give life. He had also confirmed His power over the elements of nature. Now He demonstrated his power to smite and destroy. The timing of such was perfect, for just a few days hence He would find Himself among his accusers, hanging on a cross. Had He so desired, He could then have easily harnessed the same power to smite his enemies and lower Himself from the cross. Perhaps His Apostles, witnessing His ability to destroy on this occasion, would more easily believe later that week that He could do so again, if the occasion warranted such action. Is it possible He acted, in part, to fortify their faith in His omnipotence?

Second, in His divine role as Savior of mankind, Jesus became the Intermediary, our Advocate with the Father, and ultimately, our Judge. The Father, who desires with all His heart that we return to His presence, sent His Son to show us

---

15 James E. Talmage, *Jesus the Christ* (Salt Lake City: Deseret Book Company, 1982), 524.

the way. Those who accept, receive, honor, and obey the Son will find everlasting life in the celestial kingdom of our God. Those who do not do so and are "not valiant in the testimony of Jesus" (D&C 76:79) will be rejected and receive a lesser reward—at most, the terrestrial kingdom. Eric D. Huntsman, author of *God So Loved the World*, summarized this principle in connection with the cursed fig tree as follows: "Just as the unfruitful tree was rejected by its Master and then withered and died, so his people risk similar destruction if they do not accept their promised King."[16] Word to the wise.

The third reason for smiting the barren fig tree might have been to emphasize the importance of avoiding a life of hypocrisy, appearing to be something on the outside when within there is found much to the contrary. The next day (Tuesday) He would censure the scribes and Pharisees as hypocrites. Certainly, and especially after His last and great sacrifice, He would want to remind His followers of the importance of possessing a "broken heart and a contrite spirit" (D&C 59:8) inside and a similarly humble, meek, and submissive countenance on the outside.

Elder McConkie reminds us that Jesus never missed an opportunity to teach. "It almost seems that everything he or his associates either saw or heard or did became a text for preaching a new and an everlasting doctrine."[17] The occasion with the fig tree was similarly instructive.

Upon arriving in Jerusalem, Christ made His way to the temple. Three years earlier, as He initiated His mortal ministry,

---

16 Eric D. Huntsman, *God So Loved the World: The Final Days of the Savior's Life* (Salt Lake City: Deseret Book, 2011), 19.
17 Bruce R. McConkie, *The Mortal Messiah: From Bethlehem to Cavalry*, vol. 3, (Salt Lake City: Deseret Book, 1980), 347.

also at Passover time, He had cleansed His Father's house of moneychangers and others who had desecrated that holy sanctuary. Again He found Himself in the same place, during the same season, witnessing the same disrespectful behavior. Righteous indignation rose within Him, and He proceeded again to overturn the tables of the moneychangers and "the seats of them that sold doves" (Mark 11:15), declaring boldly, "Is it not written, My house shall be called of all nations the house of prayer? but ye have made it a den of thieves" (Mark 11:17). The Apostle John, quoting Psalm 69:9, gives meaning and motivation to Christ's forceful, indignant response in the temple, "The zeal of thine house hath eaten me up" (John 2:17).

Note the progression. Three years earlier, before He had begun to declare Himself the very Messiah, Christ had referred to the temple as "my Father's house" (John 2:16). Now that He was nearing the end of His ministry and had openly proclaimed his holy Messiahship and His oneness with the Father, He called the temple "My house" (Mark 11:17). Later in the week, after prophesying the imminent destruction of the temple and the city of Jerusalem, He would refer to the temple as "your house" and declare, it "is left unto you desolate" (Matthew 23:38).

In Book 1, chapter 29, of Elder Bruce R. McConkie's masterful work *The Mortal Messiah*, he describes the filthiness and evil that pervaded that holy place at the time of the first cleansing. He said,

> The noise and the haggling destroyed every vestige of reverence; the lowing of cattle and the bleating of sheep drowned out the

priestly performances nearby; and the filth and stench of the barnyard so overpowered the senses that arriving pilgrims soon lost the desire to worship the Lord in Spirit and in truth. It was a scene of desecration, of physical filth, and of spiritual degeneracy.[18]

The appearance and spirit of the temple on the second occasion, unfortunately, was likely much the same.

Drawing near the end of His mortal life, Jesus once again powerfully emphasized the need for reverence and respect for sacred things, especially the respect that was owed the house of the Lord. He knew of the spiritual power that could come into the life of a devoted disciple as he or she humbly sought divine guidance, strength, and peace by worshiping in the Lord's house. We likewise need the power that comes by so doing. (Prayerful study of Elder John A. Widtsoe's timeless message entitled *Temple Worship*[19] and Elder Boyd K. Packer's book *The Holy Temple* will likely bring into the heart and mind of the reader greater understanding regarding the connection between temple worship and personal sanctification.)

Furthermore, through temple worthiness and worship, we seek to qualify for a most magnificent promise made by the Lord in a revelation to the Prophet Joseph Smith in the latter days when He said, "And inasmuch as my people build a house unto me in the name of the Lord, and do not suffer any unclean thing to come into it, that it be not defiled, my

---

[18] Bruce R. McConkie, *The Mortal Messiah: From Bethlehem to Cavalry*, vol. 1, (Salt Lake City: Deseret Book, 1979), 459.

[19] John A. Widtsoe, "Temple Worship," in *The Utah Genealogical and Historical Magazine*, vol. 12, ed. Nephi Anderson, (Salt Lake City: The Deseret New Press, 1921), 49–64.

glory shall rest upon it; Yea, and my presence shall be there, for I will come into it, and *all the pure in heart that shall come into it shall see God*" (D&C 97:15–16; emphasis added). Speaking of this most sacred of experiences and the potential connection between the experience and the temple, Elder Melvin J. Ballard told of an unforgettable dream he had in which the above-mentioned promise was fulfilled.

> I found myself one evening in the dreams of the night in that sacred building, the temple. After a season of prayer and rejoicing I was informed that I should have the privilege of entering into one of those rooms, to meet a glorious personage, and, as I entered the door, I saw, seated on a raised platform, the most glorious being my eyes have ever beheld or that I ever conceived existed in all the eternal worlds. As I approached to be introduced, He arose and stepped towards me with extended arms, and He smiled as He softly spoke my name. If I shall live to be a million years old, I shall never forget that smile. He took me into His arms and kissed me, pressed me to His bosom, and blessed me, until the marrow of my bones seemed to melt! When He had finished, I fell at His feet, and, as I bathed them with my tears and kisses, I saw the prints of the nails in the feet of the Redeemer of the world. The feeling that I had in the presence of Him who hath all things in His hands, to have His love, His

> affection, and His blessing was such that if I
> can receive that of which I had but a foretaste,
> I would give all that I am, all that I ever hope
> to be, to feel what I then felt![20]

The Jews, over centuries, had become so focused on the outward appearance and detailed observance of the law that they missed the purpose and meaning of the law and the sanctifying power that comes through Christ and Christ-focused worship. The jots and tittles had become more important than the spiritual grandeur, majesty, and power found in sacred places; sacred ordinances; and quiet, heartfelt, soul-expanding, sacred worship.

On both occasions when Christ cleansed the temple, He knew that never, never could his disciples receive these sacred blessings and promises when the place was so defiled and devoid of the Spirit. He always desires that we receive His blessings. On that occasion, He did what was needed to restore an element of cleanliness and spirituality so the sincere worshipper might be rewarded.

The words of the hymn "God Is in His Holy Temple" speak beautifully of the spirit, power, and divine presence that can be found in God's holy house by reverent seekers of truth.

> God is in his holy temple.
> Earthly thoughts, be silent now,
> While with rev'rence we assemble
> And before his presence bow.
> He is with us, now and ever,

---

[20] Bryant S. Hinckley, *Sermons and Missionary Services of Melvin Joseph Ballard* (Salt Lake City: Deseret Book Company, 1949), 147–57.

> When we call upon his name,
> Aiding ev'ry good endeavor,
> Guiding ev'ry upward aim.
>
> God is in his holy temple,
> In the pure and holy mind,
> In the rev'rent heart and simple,
> In the soul from sin refined.
> Banish then each base emotion.
> Lift us up, O Lord, to thee;
> Let our souls, in pure devotion,
> Temples for thy worship be.[21]

After restoring calm and proper authority to the situation and as the Spirit of God once again rested upon that sacred place, Jesus began healing the blind and the lame who naturally gathered around Him. Then, with His mortal life nearing its end, even children seemed to perceive more clearly His divinity. These spiritually perceptive innocent ones who were present and witnessed the proceedings began praising, "Hosanna to the Son of David" (Matthew 21:15). Jewish officials who stood nearby, and in whose hearts a spirit of darkness continued to grow, demanded of Jesus, "Hearest thou what these say?" Christ's perfect reply was, "Yea; have ye never read, Out of the mouth of babes and sucklings thou hast perfected praise?" (Matthew 21:16). Our Savior, who possessed the ability to communicate volumes in a simple phrase, put His antagonists in their proper place and again implied His role as the Messiah. Elder Talmage summarized the feelings that were nearly erupting in the hearts of His accusers:

---

21 "God Is in His Holy Temple," *Hymns*, no. 132.

From Palm Sunday to Easter Sunday

> The anger of the chief priests and scribes was raging against Him; but it was impotent. They had decreed His death, and had made repeated efforts to take Him, and there He sat within the very area over which they claimed supreme jurisdiction, and they were afraid to touch Him because of the common people, whom they professed to despise yet heartily feared—"for all the people were very attentive to hear him."[22]

While the chief priests were visibly infuriated, they could do nothing against Him in such a public place where so many revered and worshipped the Lord.

Insight into the anger, rage, and resentment of the chief priests and scribes was once explained as follows:

> The chief priests were the guardians of the temple and, in fact, guardians (as they supposed) of the whole structure of Jewish religion. They glutted themselves on the profits from temple business, and so the temple was not just the source of their favored social position (which they coveted so jealously) but also the source of their incomes—more, their fortunes . . .[23]

---

22 James E. Talmage, *Jesus the Christ* (Salt Lake City: Deseret Book Company, 1982), 528–29.
23 *The Life and Teachings of Jesus and His Apostles, 2nd ed.*, (Salt Lake City: The Church of Jesus Christ of Latter-day Saints, 1978), p. 143.

The anger crescendoed in intensity in the hearts of these men but would not reach its climax until a few days thence.

While the spirit-filled followers of Christ rejoiced in His presence and benefited from His healing power, the chief priests and elders, filled with an opposing spirit, gathered again to determine how "they might halt the tide of popular acclaim now attending the ministry of this Galilean rebel, this disturber of the Mosaic order, this Rabbi from Nazareth who would destroy their craft."[24] Always there is opposition (2 Nephi 2:11). Christ forever seeks to build, lift, edify, instruct, bless, and inspire, while others seek to discredit, tear down, mock, invalidate, and destroy.

The second day of Holy Week was nearly over, and Jesus made His way, those two dusty miles, to Bethany, where He rested and prepared for what was to be an eventful, lengthy, and demanding Tuesday.

Questions to Ponder
- The need for humility instead of hypocrisy is important for all. President Ezra Taft Benson called pride "the universal sin."[25] Elder Dieter F. Uchtdorf labeled it a "sin of comparison" and a "switch that turns off . . . power."[26] Where in your life do you see the need for greater humility? How can the Savior Himself and His example help you accomplish changes for greater humility?
- There are three important questions (emphasized in italics) toward the end of the following poem by Charles Franklin

---

24 Bruce R. McConkie, *The Mortal Messiah: From Bethlehem to Calvary*, vol. 3, (Salt Lake City: Deseret Book Company, 1980), 351.
25 Ezra Taft Benson, "Cleansing the Inner Vessel," *Ensign*, May 1986, 6–7.
26 Dieter F. Uchtdorf, "Pride and the Priesthood," *Ensign* or *Liahona*, Nov. 2010, 55.

Benvegar that warrant humble reflection and relate to the stark behavioral differences between Christ and the Jewish rulers displayed during Day Two (Monday).

> I watched them tearing a building down,
> A gang of men in a busy town.
> With a ho-heave-ho and lusty yell,
> They swung a beam and a sidewall fell.
> I asked the foreman, "Are these men skilled,
> As the men you'd hire if you had to build?"
> He gave me a laugh and said, "No, indeed!
> Just common labor is all I need.
> I can easily wreck in a day or two
> What builders have taken a year to do."
> And I tho't to myself as I went my way,
> *Which of these two roles have I tried to play?*
> *Am I a builder who works with care,*
> *Measuring life by the rule and square?*
> Am I shaping my deeds by a well-made plan,
> Patiently doing the best I can?
> *Or am I a wrecker who walks the town,*
> *Content with the labor of tearing down?*[27]

- Are you regularly attending and benefiting from the sanctifying power of the temple? What changes do you see occurring over the course of your life that testify of this sanctifying influence? What changes still need to occur?

---

[27] Charles Franklin Benvegar, "The Wreckers," in *The Songs of the Free State Bards*, (New World Books, 1967), 7.

Day Three
TUESDAY

CHAPTER PREVIEW

It was Tuesday, and our Savior's mortal life on Earth was quickly coming to an end. However, He knew He had one more very full and demanding day of activity and teaching in Jerusalem that awaited Him. There was blatant hypocrisy to condemn, and there were reproving parables to teach, foreboding prophecies to pronounce, and stern warnings to give. He spoke with unmistakable clarity to the priests and teachers of their pride and hypocrisy, but no one can doubt His righteous, love-filled motivations for doing so. How He must have longed for their hearts to be equal to that of the widow whose consecrated offering would be made on this day. The crescendo between Christ and the Jewish leaders spoken of toward the end of chapter two continued to intensify on Tuesday. These spiritually blinded and hypocritical men sought ceaselessly on this day to entrap, confound, discredit, and ultimately destroy the Savior, while Jesus did all in His power to help them see clearly their duplicity and repent. The proverbial battle between good and evil was so often apparent on this day. During their return to Bethany, Jesus and His Apostles lingered on the Mount of Olives as Christ spoke openly of the coming destruction of Jerusalem and the signs of His Second Coming. While record of His activities the following day, Wednesday, is virtually nonexistent, Elder James E. Talmage devoted sixty of the nearly eight hundred pages in Jesus the Christ to this one day, Tuesday.

After Jesus journeyed from Bethany to Jerusalem and entered the temple with the Twelve, the scribes and other religious leaders approached the Savior aggressively, questioning the authority with which He had cleansed the temple on the previous day. Their intent was far from genuine and honest. They sought desperately to catch Him in His words, to confound Him, to justify a reason to take Him and condemn Him to death.

Their first question was, "by what authority doest thou these things?" (Luke 20:2). Wisely He responded with a question of His own: "The baptism of John, was it from heaven, or of men?" (Luke 20:4). They could not reply. If they suggested John acted with legitimate authority from God, Jesus would ask why then they had not accepted his teachings and his baptism. However, if they questioned John's authority, the multitude that was present and continued holding the deceased John the Baptist as a great prophet sent from God would turn against them. They answered Jesus "that they could not tell" (Luke 20:7), to which Jesus replied, "Neither tell I you by what authority I do these things" (Luke 20:8). Certainly the Savior possessed all of the great gifts of the Spirit, but one in particular—the gift of discernment—He would use extensively that day.

Christ then took opportunity to share three parables that further and directly denounced these wicked priests. We must remember that Christ's primary motivation was and is always love. Certainly His desire was for the unrighteous rulers to repent. However, He knew the opposite was likely. Picture in your mind the escalating tension between the Jewish leaders and Jesus as the poignant parables described below were shared. Imagine the large gathering of onlookers and the scribes and Pharisees being subtly rebuked but having nowhere to escape. (You may choose to read the parables referenced for further emphasis.)

Parable of the Two Sons (Matthew 21:28–32)
In this parable Jesus said it would be so much easier for repentant publicans and harlots to enter the kingdom of God than these unrepentant Jewish rulers.

Parable of the Wicked Husbandmen (Luke 20:9–18)
In this parable Jesus likened these wicked leaders to the husbandmen who beat and killed the servants (prophets) and even the very son (Jesus) of the lord of the vineyard. Following this parable, Jesus spoke rather openly that He was the stone, "which the builders rejected" that became the "head of the corner." He also proclaimed that the kingdom of God would be taken from them, the children of Abraham, and given to another nation (the gentiles, to whom the Apostles would eventually preach the gospel following Christ's ascension). This clearly infuriated the priests, but Christ's time had not yet come.

Parable of the Marriage of the King's Son (Matthew 22:2–10)

In this parable the king prepared a great feast and sent his servants (the prophets) to call those that were bidden (the house of Israel) to come, but they would not. So, the servants went into the highway and gathered all who would respond to the invitation (the gentiles).

Summarizing these parables, Elder Talmage said, "even the children of the covenant will be rejected except they make good their title by godly works."[28]

While often our Savior would couch truths and doctrine in parables to protect the spiritually unprepared, on this occasion we assume He must have known the intended audience would perfectly grasp the true meaning of His message and that that message would sear their hearts like a hot iron. Jesus always spoke truth, motivated by love. This He did, knowing at times—like the one that necessitated the parables—that truth spoken to hard hearts may unfortunately result in anger, not humility and change. But speak He must, hoping that maybe, just maybe, repentance would be the result. These were the last parables the Savior would teach in public. A few others were shared later on that Tuesday, but only with His beloved Apostles.

Still attempting to entrap Him, the Pharisees and Herodians asked Jesus, "Is it lawful to give tribute unto Caesar, or not?" (Matthew 22:17). If Jesus answered yes, the people who endlessly encircled Him and were fierce opponents of

---

28 James E. Talmage, *Jesus the Christ* (Salt Lake City: Deseret Book Company, 1982), 540.

Roman rule may have suggested He was disloyal to Abraham. But if He answered no, the Herodians may have suggested He was encouraging sedition against the Roman government. Jesus, again, refused to allow Himself to be ensnared. He responded, "Why tempt ye me, ye hypocrites?" (Matthew 22:18). Then, calling for a Roman denarius (coin) equal to the value of one day's wages, He noted the image of Caesar on the surface and astutely said, "Render therefore unto Caesar the things which are Caesar's; and unto God the things that are God's" (Matthew 22:21). Masterful!

Next the Pharisees—who had for so many years parsed, segmented, and defined in the minutest detail the law of Moses—asked, "Master, which is the great commandment in the law?" (Matthew 22:36), trying to use this ploy to deceive and trick Jesus, believing that no one understood the law as well as them. The Savior's reply, which has attracted the admiration of Christian theologians for centuries, was, "Thou shalt love the Lord thy God with all thy heart, and with all thy soul, and with all thy mind. This is the first and great commandment. And the second is like unto it, Thou shalt love thy neighbor as thyself. On these two commandments hang all the law and the prophets" (Matthew 22:37–40). Even the scribe who asked the question, hoping to mislead Jesus, was noticeably caught off guard and implied agreement when he said, "Well, Master, thou hast said the truth" (Mark 12:32). One can almost imagine Jesus winking at the man when the Savior responded, "Thou art not far from the kingdom of God" (Mark 12:34).

Though He had effectively silenced His accusers who sought to entangle Him, Jesus knew He still was not done. He needed to condemn the blatant hypocrisy of the scribes and Pharisees for at least two possible reasons. First, as always, to give them a chance to repent by seeing clearly their own duplicity. Elder D. Todd Christofferson taught, "Surely no one would accuse the Savior of not loving these scribes and Pharisees—after all, He suffered and died to save them too. But loving them, He could not let them go on in sin without clearly correcting them."[29] The second likely reason for explicitly censuring the scribes and Pharisees was to establish clearly for all the importance of ensuring congruity between what is perceived on the outside of a person and the spirit that dwells within.

He first spoke to and warned His disciples and the multitude, intentionally within earshot of His enemies, by saying, "All therefore whatsoever they bid you observe, that observe and do; but do not ye after their works: for they say, and do not" (Matthew 23:3). Or in modern vernacular, "Do as they say, not as they do." He continued, "But all their works they do for to be seen of men" (Matthew 23:5). As suggested above, the Savior was both calling the eavesdroppers to repentance and teaching the future leaders of His Church that "he that is greatest among you shall be your servant" (Matthew 23:11), as He had perfectly epitomized throughout His mortal ministry.

Imagine the anger that was continuing to build among the Jewish leaders. But that was just the beginning. Jesus went on to pronounce the following woes on the hypocritical scribes and Pharisees:

---

29 D. Todd Christofferson, "The Voice of Warning," *Ensign* or *Liahona*, May 2017, 109.

- "Woe unto you, scribes and Pharisees, hypocrites! for ye devour widows' houses [by the excessive collection of money], and for a pretence make long prayer: therefore ye shall receive the greater damnation" (Matthew 23:14).
- "Woe unto you, scribes and Pharisees, hypocrites! for ye pay tithe of mint and anise and cummin, and have omitted the weightier matters of the law, judgment, mercy, and faith: these ought ye to have done, and not to leave the other undone. Ye blind guides, which strain at a gnat, and swallow a camel" (Matthew 23:23–24).
- "Woe unto you, scribes and Pharisees, hypocrites! for ye make clean the outside of the cup and of the platter, but within they are full of extortion and excess" (Matthew 23:25).
- "Woe unto you, scribes and Pharisees, hypocrites! for ye are like unto whited sepulchres, which indeed appear beautiful outward, but are within full of dead men's bones, and of all uncleanness. Even so ye also outwardly appear righteous unto men, but within ye are full of hypocrisy and iniquity" (Matthew 23:27–28).
- "Woe unto you, scribes and Pharisees, hypocrites! because ye build the tombs of the prophets, and garnish the sepulchres of the righteous, And say, If we had been in the days of our fathers, we would not have been partakers with them in the blood of the prophets" (Matthew 23:29-30).

Jesus's wholly justifiable denunciation of the Jewish rulers had ended. They had become hypocrites, believing they were the very authority of the Mosaic law given to them by their revered Jehovah, and had become so blinded that they could not even recognize Him when Jehovah Himself stood in their presence. And worse, soon they would demand that the very Jehovah, He who had come as their Messiah and Savior, be crucified.

Thinking of all He had done during His ministry, and specifically on this day, to reclaim wayward Israel and especially their errant leaders, Jesus gazed out over the city and lamented, "O Jerusalem, Jerusalem, thou that killest the prophets, and stonest them which are sent unto thee, how often would I have gathered thy children together, even as a hen gathereth her chickens under her wings, and ye would not!" (Matthew 23:37). For three years Christ had genuinely and lovingly tried to gather His people (the tribe of Judah and, more broadly, the House of Israel), but the hardened hearts of so many had prevented them from recognizing and accepting Him as their Master.

Moving toward the treasury, Jesus observed the people passing thirteen chests that were properly placed to receive monetary contributions. It was here He saw both rich and poor making their offerings as mandated by religious law, some of their abundance and others of their scarcity. The most noticeable, however, was a certain widow who deposited two mites, representing "all her living" (Mark 12:44). Elder Talmage described the scene thus: "The rich gave much yet kept back more; the widow's gift was her all."[30] As Christ would perfectly demonstrate later that week, discipleship requires a similar commitment from all who choose to follow Him.

As Jesus departed the temple precincts, one of His disciples commented on the majesty and magnificence of

---

30 James E. Talmage, *Jesus the Christ* (Salt Lake City: Deseret Book Company, 1982), 561.

the structure. The Lord remarked, "verily I say unto you, There shall not be left here one stone upon another, that shall not be thrown down" (Matthew 24:2). He was referring, of course, to the complete destruction of Jerusalem, including the temple, which would occur within four short decades.

This prophesy caught His Apostles' attention and was the subject of much discussion and instruction when they reached a certain place on the Mount of Olives during their final return to Bethany. There on the Mount, one of the Apostles asked, "Tell us, when shall these things be? and what shall be the sign of thy coming, and of the end of the world?" (Matthew 24:3). Jesus began teaching them of things that would occur in the near-term as well as of things that would transpire in the distant future.

As He sat with His Apostles on the hillside, Jesus first counseled them to expect persecution because of their testimony of Him, the Christ. While He said they would suffer even unto death, He also reassured them of their eternal welfare.

He then told them of the "abomination of desolation" (Mark 13:14) to which He had made reference earlier in the temple. The prophet Daniel had anciently prophesied this destruction. Elder McConkie spoke as follows of both the "abomination of desolation" that occurred in 70 A.D. and of the destruction that will occur prior to the Savior's Second Coming:

> All the desolation and waste which attended the former destruction of Jerusalem is but prelude to the coming siege. Titus and his legions slaughtered 1,100,000 Jews,

> destroyed the temple, and ploughed the city. In the coming reenactment of this "abomination of desolation," the whole world will be at war, Jerusalem will be the center of the conflict, every modern weapon will be used, and in the midst of the siege the Son of Man shall come, setting his foot upon the mount of Olives and fighting the battle of His saints.[31]

Imagine the Apostles sitting there overlooking beautiful Jerusalem and being told that not many years hence, within their own lifetimes, the scene would change to one of destruction, devastation, and ruin.

Next, Jesus prophesied the fate of the Jews, from their imminent scattering to their eventual gathering in the latter days. He prophesied the Great Apostasy that would occur when Satan, the prince of darkness, would deceive and confound many through the spreading of false doctrine. The Savior also prophesied His own Second Coming with these words: "For as the lightning cometh out of the east, and shineth even unto the west; so shall also the coming of the Son of man be" (Matthew 24:27), but not before "the sun be darkened, and the moon shall not give her light, and the stars shall fall from heaven" (Matthew 24:29).

While continuing to speak to His Apostles, Jesus also spoke indirectly to us, as if we were present, admonishing us to "watch." Specifically He warned, "Lest coming suddenly he find you sleeping. And what I say unto you I say unto

---

31 Bruce R. McConkie, *Doctrinal New Testament Commentary: The Gospels*, vol. 1, (Salt Lake City: Bookcraft, Inc., 1976), 659.

all, Watch" (Mark 13:36–37). He emphasized His counsel by sharing the timeless parable of the ten virgins (Matthew 25:1–13), in which five wise and five foolish virgins awaited the coming of the bridegroom. The five wise virgins, as it says in the Doctrine and Covenants, "received the truth, [took] the Holy Spirit for their guide, and [were] not . . . deceived" (D&C 45:57). Such wise counsel in any day, but especially for us, who live in the latter days!

Christ then delivered the parable of the talents (Matthew 25:14–30), which tells of "a man traveling into a far country, who called his own servants, and delivered unto them his goods," five talents to one, two talents to another, and one talent to the last. When the traveler returned, he asked for an accounting. The servant with five had multiplied them and returned ten. The one with two had also multiplied them and returned four. But the last, with one talent, did nothing to further develop it and returned only one. The first and second servants were equally rewarded, while the last servant's talent was taken away.

One interpretation of this parable is that we all have talents and have been commanded to develop and use those talents for the benefit of God's work and the building of His Kingdom. Those who do so, even though some may have received more talents initially than others, will receive the same Celestial reward. On the other hand, those who receive talents and fail to develop and contribute them to the Lord's storehouse (D&C 82:18) for the benefit of His work and His children, will lose the talents they received and will fail to qualify for exaltation.

Jesus's concluding instruction to His Apostles as they sat on the Mount of Olives on that Tuesday afternoon made reference first to the eventual judgment when the Lord will separate His sheep from the goats, setting "the sheep on his right hand, but the goats on the left" (Matthew 25:33). The famous standard against which true discipleship has ever since been measured was then given when the Lord Jesus Christ said,

> Then shall the King say unto them on his right hand, Come, ye blessed of my Father, inherit the kingdom prepared for you from the foundation of the world: For I was an hungered, and ye gave me meat: I was thirsty, and ye gave me drink: I was a stranger, and ye took me in: Naked, and ye clothed me: I was sick, and ye visited me: I was in prison, and ye came unto me.
>
> Then shall the righteous answer him, saying, Lord, when saw we thee an hungred, and fed thee? or thirsty, and gave thee drink? When saw we thee a stranger, and took thee in? or naked, and clothed thee? Or when saw we thee sick, or in prison, and came unto thee?
>
> And the King shall answer and say unto them, Verily I say unto you, Inasmuch as ye have done it unto one of the least of these my brethren, ye have done it unto me. (Matthew 25:34–40)

Such timeless tutelage! Imagine sitting at the feet of the Master, being instructed as to things that will come and how best to prepare. Fortunately, we are similarly instructed in our day as we listen to, cherish, and obey the words of living prophets. Theirs, too, is equally timeless tutelage.

Christ spent much of that Tuesday calling the scribes, Pharisees, and other Jewish leaders to repentance because of their hard-hearted, pride-filled, hypocritical natures and warning everyone of the destruction that would come upon the Jews then and the unrighteous at His Second Coming. The message of Tuesday is clear and unmistakable, and one that emphasizes the constant and enduring need for humility and holiness. Consider and reflect often on the words of the hymn "More Holiness Give Me," written as a plea to God for His help to overcome the weaknesses of the flesh and become more like the Savior:

> More holiness give me,
> More strivings within,
> More patience in suff'ring,
> More sorrow for sin,
> More faith in my Savior,
> More sense of his care,
> More joy in his service,
> More purpose in prayer.
>
> More gratitude give me,
> More trust in the Lord,
> More pride in his glory,
> More hope in his word,
> More tears for his sorrows,
> More pain at his grief,
> More meekness in trial,
> More praise for relief.

> More purity give me,
> More strength to o'ercome,
> More freedom from earth-stains,
> More longing for home.
> More fit for the kingdom,
> More used would I be,
> More blessed and holy—
> More, Savior, like thee.[32]

Jesus and His Apostles completed their journey to Bethany. Somewhere along the way He reminded them, "Ye know that after two days is the feast of the passover, and the Son of man is betrayed to be crucified" (Matthew 26:2). Perhaps they walked in foreboding silence the remainder of their journey, contemplating what awaited their Master and perhaps what might await them.

Questions to Ponder

- In this chapter, Christ demonstrated the gift of discernment, which He used perfectly to avoid being ensnared by the wicked Jewish rulers. What gifts of the Spirit do you possess? Given your own weaknesses, what additional gifts of the Spirit would you like to seek after and receive? How will you go about developing them?
- Though always motivated by love, sometimes Christ's corrections of the hard-hearted resulted in anger, not the desired change. When you are lovingly corrected, do you resist, or do you accept with a spirit of meekness, humility, and willingness to change?
- Jesus taught that the great commandment is to love God and our fellowmen. What evidence suggests you

---

32 "More Holiness Give Me," *Hymns*, no. 131.

should seek to observe that all-important commandment in your life? What opportunities are there to further strengthen obedience to this commandment?
- The widow who cast in two mites gave her all. How willing and ready are you to give your all to Christ and to the work of His kingdom?
- President Thomas S. Monson often spoke of the need to go to the rescue.[33] On this last Tuesday of Christ's mortal life, Christ spoke of a similar need to feed the hungry, give drink to the thirsty, care for the stranger, clothe the naked, and minister unto the sick and those imprisoned (physically, spiritually, mentally, or emotionally). How does the Spirit suggest you should be about this great rescuing work?
- As the Second Coming approaches, what efforts are you making to "watch" and be ready?

---

33 Thomas S. Monson, "To the Rescue," *Ensign*, May 2001.

Day Four
WEDNESDAY

CHAPTER PREVIEW

There appears to be little or no written record of that which the Savior did on the final Wednesday of His mortal life, though it was likely spent in Bethany among His closest friends and associates. He may have felt the need to recover from an emotionally exhausting Tuesday and to prepare for what awaited Him during His last two days of mortality. While a brief respite may benefit the reader as well in preparation for an agonizing Thursday, reflecting for a few precious minutes on how Jesus might have spent this day causes a few possibilities to come to mind that may be worthy of consideration.

One can certainly imagine that Christ spent a portion of Wednesday in private, removed from outward influences, in quiet contemplation and prayer to His Father. He often demonstrated the need for spiritual preparation during His life and would frequently remove Himself for lengthy periods of time to pray. One example occurred at the beginning of His mortal ministry when He fasted and prayed for forty days

(Matthew 4:2). Another occurred when He departed from the multitude after feeding and preaching to thousands and "went up into a mountain apart to pray" (Matthew 14:23). Knowing the excruciating pain, trials, and challenges that lay ahead, He must have felt that His spirit needed to be as strong and resilient as possible in order to succeed and triumph. He had come to Earth for the sole purpose of fulfilling the will of His Father and certainly had no intention of leaving mortality having done anything less than perfectly fulfilling every word of command.

Perhaps, additionally, our Lord sought to counter somber feelings accompanying contemplation of the events that awaited Him, by pondering the glorious Resurrection that would soon occur and the opportunity to return to the loving arms of His Holy Father. In Hebrews 12:2 the Apostle Paul speaks clearly of the Savior's ability to endure the Atonement by focusing on "the joy that was set before him." All would do well to adopt such a wise practice!

Our Master may also have spent time with the future leaders of His Church, giving final counsel and instruction. Just as the Prophet Joseph Smith, during his final days and weeks in mortality, spent an increasing amount of time preparing and giving instruction to those latter-day Apostles, Jesus may likely have done the same. Much had been accomplished in the past three years to replace, in the minds of His Apostles, the "traditions of the fathers" with the doctrine of the law of the celestial kingdom. On that Wednesday, one can imagine Christ ensuring that the principles He had taught were understood and the governance of His Church was well established. Of course,

He knew His cherished Apostles would continue to receive heavenly tutelage through the intermediary of the Holy Ghost, but the Savior likely felt the need, during these final hours, to provide all the instruction, counsel, direction, and reassurance He could.

Finally, given the Savior's perfect disposition to always turn outward, it can be supposed that He gathered His loved ones and dearest friends and associates around Him to give them encouragement and strength. He knew of the persecutions that awaited those who would proclaim devotion to Him as Messiah and Savior of the world. When imagining how tender His feelings must have been for those He loved and who loved Him, it is easy to believe He did all He could to prepare them.

There are myriad examples of individuals who gave blessings to family and close friends before their departure from mortality. Lehi gathered and blessed his posterity (2 Nephi 4:12), as did Jacob, whose name was changed to Israel (Genesis 49). Countless are the fathers who call their families together and do the same before their passing. Similarly, many loving mothers, before departing this life, gather their children and grandchildren around their beds, give tender counsel, and share the affectionate feelings of their hearts, all for the purpose of lifting and encouraging those they love. It stands to reason that Jesus, who loved perfectly, would desire with all His heart to offer words of uplifting reassurance and perhaps even lay His loving hands on the heads of his beloved mother; the Twelve; his dear friends Mary, Martha, and Lazarus; and perhaps others, and bestow precious blessings upon them.

Of the Savior's outward focus and ministering approach to life, Elder David A. Bednar made an insightful comparison between Matthew 4:11 as found in the King James Version of the Bible and the same verse in the Joseph Smith Translation. As background to that verse, Jesus had just completed a physically agonizing, yet spiritually enriching, forty-day fast and had successfully withstood the temptations of the devil. In the King James Version of Matthew 4:11 we read, "Then the devil leaveth him, and, behold, angels came and ministered unto him." However, in the Joseph Smith Translation the angels' ministry appears to have been directed elsewhere. We read, "Then the devil leaveth him, and, now Jesus knew that John was cast into prison, and he sent angels, and, behold, they came and ministered unto [John]." Though one could easily argue that the Savior would have appreciated the ministering influence of angels after having completed such a fast and endured Satan's temptations, Jesus's attention was then, as always, on the needs of others. In this case, it was focused on John the Baptist, who had been falsely accused and imprisoned at the behest of Herod.[34]

Jesus's character was such that on Wednesday, the day before He would suffer immeasurably in the Garden of Gethsemane, His thoughts would not turn inward but would remain focused on those He came to serve, then and throughout all eternity. Anything He may have done to increase His own strength was likely done to ensure that He, in the end, came off conqueror for the benefit of all of God's children, including you and me.

Though we do not know exactly how Wednesday was spent, we do know one thing: it was well spent, as had

---

34 David A. Bednar, "Exceedingly Valiant for Courage," [Brigham Young University—Idaho commencement, Jan. 25, 2003], byui.edu.

From Palm Sunday to Easter Sunday

been every other day of His thirty-three short years of life on Earth. Despite His own mournful situation, given the events that would soon transpire, one can vividly picture Jesus continuing to love, lift, serve, and bless.

The simple words of the hymn "Love One Another" capture the feelings that must have been present in abundance on that day, the love Christ invites all to share.

> As I have loved you,
> Love one another.
> This new commandment:
> Love one another.
> By this shall men know
> Ye are my disciples,
> If ye have love
> One to another.[35]

Questions to Ponder

- How else do you feel the Savior might have spent this important day of His life?
- When you arrive at the end of mortality, how will you want to spend your precious final days? What can you do now with those you love, though your passing may still be distant?
- With regard to the concept of living a life with an outward focus, what opportunities do you see in your own life to do more of this?

---

35 "Love One Another" by Luacine Clark Fox/ arr. by Jo Marie Borgeson Bray © by Intellectual Reserve, Inc., *Hymns*, no. 308.

Day Five
THURSDAY

CHAPTER PREVIEW

The time foretold by all ancient prophets, and one of the most critical days anticipated before the world was, had arrived. Whether the world and all of God's creations would forever remain in their fallen state or possess the hope of everlasting life and exaltation would be determined by the outcome of this day's events and those to follow through Sunday. On this incomparable day, much would be done. The Passover supper, with the new and sacred ordinances of the sacrament and the washing of the Apostles' feet, would be given. Christ would teach gospel principles of the highest order, such as: "love one another; as I have loved you" (John 13:34); trust that "In my Father's house are many mansions" and "I go to prepare a place for you" (John 14:2); accept that "I am the vine, ye are the branches" (John 15:5); understand that the greatest expression of love to God is to "keep [His] commandments" (John 14:15); receive, cherish, and obey the voice of the Comforter (John 15:26); seek after yet "another Comforter" (John 14:16); and acknowledge that "Greater love hath no man than [to] lay down his life for his friends" (John

15:13). The most beautiful example of heartfelt, sincere, love-filled prayer to the Father on behalf of others would be offered (John 17). Finally the most selfless, far-reaching act of love ever undertaken in human history would be wrought in a garden called Gethsemane.

ON THURSDAY THE EVENTS COMPOSING Christ's Atonement, including the suffering, the Crucifixion, and His subsequent Resurrection and Ascension, began. He had been foreordained and prepared for this moment from the great Council in Heaven, when He offered to come to Earth and atone for all mankind. The time had come, and as always, He moved decisively forward with great conviction, full of faith, nothing wavering, and with no intention of shirking or shrinking. His determination to accomplish the will of His Father and the equal determination of the Jewish leaders to have Him killed would soon collide, all for an eternal, soul-saving purpose.

While Jesus was making arrangements for the Passover supper with His Apostles, the conspiratorial Judas Iscariot was finalizing an arrangement of his own. He, an entirely unexpected ally, agreed with the Jewish leaders to privately betray Jesus that very night. The price of the deed was thirty pieces of silver, the same price that would have then been paid for a slave.[36] With selfish, hate-filled hearts, the rulers and Judas made an accord.

In the meantime, Peter and John had been instructed by their Master, who again demonstrated His gift of seership, to return to Jerusalem, where they would encounter a man carrying a pitcher of water. They were to follow him into his

---

36 James E. Talmage, *Jesus the Christ* (Salt Lake City: Deseret Book Company, 1982), 614–15.

house and ask where Jesus and His disciples were to eat the Passover. They would be shown to a large upper room where they were to make all things ready for that evening.

At the appointed hour, Jesus and the Twelve gathered in the upper room for the last meal the Lord would eat in mortality. Many of the common traditions of the Passover were observed, amidst what must have been a spirit of noticeable and understandable sadness. These feelings of melancholy must have been especially evident at the moment Jesus announced that one present would betray Him that very evening. The record suggests that the Twelve humbly and instinctively asked, "Lord, is it I?" (Matthew 26:22). Judas Iscariot, perhaps not wanting to be perceived as different, also said, "Master, is it I?" to which the Savior responded, "Thou hast said" (Matthew 26:25).

The next occurrence of significance was the introduction of the Priesthood ordinance of the washing of feet, which has again been performed in our day, beginning at the School of the Prophets in Kirtland. When Jesus offered to wash Peter's feet, Peter protested, after which Jesus explained, "If I wash thee not, thou hast no part with me" (John 13:8). Of course, Peter conceded.

After completing this sacred ordinance on behalf of all the Apostles, Jesus said, "ye are clean, but not all" (John 13:10), referring, of course, to Judas Iscariot, for whom no amount of washing at that time could cleanse his sinful heart.

Another sacred Priesthood ordinance was then instituted; one that has been administered literally millions of times since and has direct reference to the blood that would be shed later that night and the body that would be offered the next day for all of Christ's disciples—past, present, and future. Of course, that ordinance is the sacrament. The bread was administered first, in remembrance of the Savior's sacrificed body, followed by the wine, in remembrance of His spilt blood. As President Russell M. Nelson taught, "We commemorate His Atonement in a very personal way. We bring a broken heart and a contrite spirit to our sacrament meeting. It is the highlight of our Sabbath-day observance."[37] Elder Melvin J. Ballard, Apostle and grandfather of current Apostle M. Russell Ballard, likewise shared his feelings about this sacred ordinance when he declared, "I am a witness that there is a spirit attending the administration of the sacrament that warms the soul from head to foot; you feel the wounds of the spirit being healed, and the load being lifted. Comfort and happiness come to the soul that is worthy and truly desirous of partaking of this spiritual food."[38] Of significance, Jesus also administered this sacred ordinance among the Nephites on the American continent and will again administer it at Adam-ondi-Ahman in connection with His Second Coming. Imagine the Spirit that must have been present in that upper room on that sacred night of the sacrament's first administration.

Whether the sacramental administration occurred prior to or following the next event is unclear in the record. Jesus reiterated that one among them would betray Him. John asked who it would be, and Jesus replied, "He it is, to whom I shall give a sop [a piece of bread dipped in some kind of mixture], when I have dipped it" (John 13:26). At this, Jesus

---

[37] Russell M. Nelson, "Worshiping at Sacrament Meeting," *Ensign* or *Liahona*, Aug. 2004.

[38] Melvin J. Ballard, *Melvin J. Ballard: Crusader for Righteousness* (Salt Lake City: Bookcraft, 1966), 132–133.

dipped and offered the bread to Judas Iscariot and then resolutely said, "That thou doest, do quickly" (John 13:27), to which Judas responded by exiting immediately, forever severing his apostolic association with his brethren and the Lord. The gift of discernment was again on full display that night as our Savior perfectly perceived the evil intent in the heart of His associate, Judas.

The mood must have been somewhat changed and the Spirit strengthened after Judas's departure and when the Savior then began to teach. Imagine being one of the remaining eleven sitting at the Savior's feet, being instructed in those things He felt were most essential before His martyrdom. With the events of the Atonement near, Christ's feelings must have been very tender. The spirit in the room had to have been palpable, the feelings of love and concern powerful, as the Apostles focused on Him, hanging on every word He uttered.

The first instruction was most fitting: "That ye love one another; as I have loved you, that ye also love one another. By this shall all men know that ye are my disciples, if ye have love one to another" (John 13:34–35). It could not be clearer. Christ had previously confirmed that the great commandment in the law was to love (the Father and one's neighbor). On this night He reiterated its importance to those who would be responsible to teach and demonstrate this everlasting principle to the world. In a few short hours, the greatest demonstration of love, the very reason John said, "For God so loved the world" (John 3:16), would be selflessly offered.

Christ then taught Peter (and all of us, indirectly) that Satan desired to "sift [him] as wheat" (Luke 22:31), but He reassured Peter that He had prayed for His Apostle "that [his] faith fail not: and when [he was] converted, [he should] strengthen [his] brethren" (Luke 22:32). The same can be said of any of His faithful followers. Christ loves us, warns us, and prays for us and then commands that when we are converted, we must reach out in that same Christlike love to strengthen others. It is what the "holier approach to caring for and ministering to others," of which President Russell M. Nelson has spoken, is all about.[39]

Next, Jesus taught that in the afterlife there are "many mansions" (John 14:2). How comforting it is to know that all will be rewarded both justly and mercifully, suited to a man or woman's individual worthiness and made possible by the Savior's grace. However, Christ not only shared the fact that "many mansions" exist but also went on to explain how to qualify for the most glorious of them all by saying, "I am the way, the truth, and the life: no man cometh unto the Father, but by me" (John 14:6). Consistent with this counsel, Jesus then taught the Apostles, "I am the vine, ye are the branches: He that abideth in me, and I in him, the same bringeth forth much fruit: for without me ye can do nothing" (John 15:5). Implicit in this instruction is the requirement that we faithfully come unto and abide in Him in order to receive the most glorious celestial reward. There is no other way.

The Savior then promised the Apostles the gift of the Holy Ghost. While He would be departing, Jesus reassured and comforted them when He said, "I will not leave you comfortless: I will come to you" (John 14:18). The Apostle John's record not only speaks of the promised Holy Ghost but of another Comforter (John 14:16). Doctrine and

---

39 Russell M. Nelson, "Ministering with the Power and Authority of God," *Ensign* or *Liahona*, May 2018, 100.

Covenants 88:3–4 also confirms the existence of another Comforter, and the Prophet Joseph Smith explained who that other Comforter is:

> Now what is this other Comforter? It is no more or less than the Lord Jesus Christ himself; & this is the sum & substance of the whole matter, that when any man obtains this last Comforter he will have the personage of Jesus Christ to attend him or appear unto him from time to time. & even he will manifest the Father unto him & they will take up their abode with him, & the visions of the heavens will be opened unto him & the Lord will teach him face to face & he may have a perfect knowledge of the mysteries of the kingdom of God.[40]

What glorious doctrine! What a magnificent promise!

Foreshadowing the events of the next day, Jesus then said, "Greater love hath no man than this, that a man lay down his life for his friends" (John 15:13). By so saying, Jesus called you and me His friends, as we accept and exercise faith in Him as Savior and Redeemer, seek to obey all of His commandments, sincerely repent when we sin, and strive diligently to "endure to the end" (1 Nephi 22:31). May we forever be worthy, by doing the things just mentioned, to be called His friends.

His final instruction to His beloved Apostles came by affirming the reality of His imminent Resurrection;

---

40 "Discourse, between circa 26 June and circa 2 July 1839, as Reported by Willard Richards," *The Joseph Smith Papers* 17 (October 2018), http://www.josephsmithpapers.org/paper-summary/discourse-between-circa-26-june-and-circa-2-july-1839-as-reported-by-willard-richards/6.

confirming, "In the world ye shall have tribulation"; encouraging them to "be of good cheer"; and reminding them with words filled with perfect faith, "I have overcome the world" (John 16:33). Implicit in His words is the reassuring thought that if Christ has overcome the world, we can as well, so long as we take Him and the Holy Spirit for our guides.

Before departing the upper room, Jesus offered one of the most sacred and heartfelt prayers ever spoken. It has come to be known as the great Intercessory Prayer, or the Lord's High Priestly Prayer (John 17). In this prayer Jesus spoke to His Father intimately, personally, and most respectfully; rendered a humble accounting of the work He had been given to do in mortality; taught that "life eternal" is to "know . . . the only true God, and Jesus Christ, whom [God hath] sent"; and affectionately and tenderly prayed that the Father would care for His Apostles and "them also which [should] believe on [Him] through their word," blessing them to become one with the Father and Himself. The spirit in the room during that prayer must have been divine!

After they had sung a hymn (note the central role of sacred music), Jesus and His remaining eleven special witnesses departed that upper room and made their way beyond the city walls to the Garden of Gethsemane, which would become sacred that night by means of what was about to occur. The name Gethsemane means oil press, or the garden of the olive press.[41] Great pressure was applied to extract oil from the olives in that very garden. On that night, however, it would be the weight of the sins and mortal afflictions of

---

41 Truman G. Madsen, "The Olive Press," *Ensign*, December 1982; Definition of "Gethsemane" on Dictionary.com, http://www.dictionary.com/browse/gethsemane.

mankind that would exert their force on our Savior, resulting in literal drops of blood flowing from His pores.

Leaving eight of the Apostles near the entrance to the garden, Jesus took Peter, James, and John farther. The weight of what was about to occur began to envelop the Lord. The scriptures say He "began to be sore amazed, and to be very heavy" (Mark 14:33). Even Jesus was "awestruck" or "astonished" (translation of "sore amazed" from the Greek)[42] at the intensity of the feelings that began to overcome Him. Speaking unto the three with Him, Jesus said, "My soul is exceeding sorrowful unto death: tarry ye here, and watch" (Mark 14:34). He proceeded a short distance farther, fell on His face and asked the Father if it was possible for the cup to pass from Him, and then lovingly and deferentially said, "nevertheless not as I will, but as thou wilt" (Matthew 26:39). He was forever, even facing the horrific agony that awaited Him, perfectly obedient to the Father's will.

What happened next no mortal, unenlightened words can adequately describe. Jesus Christ, the Savior of the world, began a process in Gethsemane that would end on the cross, whereby He would voluntarily suffer for the sins of all of God's children—past, present, and future. Not only would He suffer for our sins but He would likewise endure every pain, illness, trial, and affliction inherent in the mortal condition (Alma 7:11–12). All of this He would experience intimately, individually, completely, and without limitation. So agonizingly painful was the experience that the Father sent "an angel unto him from heaven, strengthening him" (Luke 22:43). Elder McConkie has suggested that the angel was

---

[42] Definition of "Astonished" on *Bible Hub*, https://biblehub.com/greek/1568.htm.

none other than father Adam.[43] He and Eve had faithfully done their part to initiate the mortal experience by partaking of the forbidden fruit. And, at that moment in the garden, Adam may have been sent by the Father to strengthen His Son who was undergoing precisely what was required to eternally overcome the effects of the Fall. Relative to His suffering in the garden and on the cross, the Savior Himself described it to the Prophet Joseph Smith as follows: "For behold, I, God, have suffered these things for all, that they might not suffer if they would repent; but if they would not repent they must suffer even as I; Which suffering caused myself, even God, the greatest of all, to tremble because of pain, and to bleed at every pore, and to suffer both body and spirit" (D&C 19:16–18).

Elder McConkie taught that Christ suffered twice: once in the Garden of Gethsemane and again on the cross.[44] I have often wondered why Jesus had to experience that torment on two separate occasions. The answer that makes the most sense to me is that what occurred in the garden, including the strengthening influence of an angel from the presence of God the Father, was preparation for what was to occur on the cross when Jesus would need to suffer all alone, even for a time without the sustaining influence of His loving Father. Elder Jeffrey R. Holland described the utter loneliness of this latter experience as follows:

> That the supreme sacrifice of His Son might be as complete as it was voluntary and

---

[43] Bruce R. McConkie, "The Purifying Power of Gethsemane," *Ensign*, May 1985.
[44] Ibid.

solitary, the Father briefly withdrew from Jesus the comfort of His Spirit, the support of His personal presence. It was required, indeed it was central to the significance of the Atonement, that this perfect Son who had never spoken ill nor done wrong nor touched an unclean thing had to know how the rest of humankind—us, all of us—would feel when we did commit such sins. For His Atonement to be infinite and eternal, He had to feel what it was like to die not only physically but spiritually, to sense what it was like to have the divine Spirit withdraw, leaving one feeling totally, abjectly, hopelessly alone.[45]

Exactly what the Savior endured during those two unfathomable experiences is not precisely known. What is known is that it was exactly enough for you, for me, and for all of God's creations.[46] His suffering was not an ounce too little. Christ paid the full and complete price, with no balance due. His eternal Atonement was wrought perfectly to bring about the opportunity for an eternal "at-one-ment" of mankind with God as the Father knew, with perfect faith, would happen when He accepted His Firstborn Son's selfless offer of redemption in the premortal Council in Heaven.

Having successfully completed this horrific but eternally essential experience, Jesus returned to his sleeping Apostles

---

[45] Jeffrey R. Holland, "None Were with Him," *Ensign* or *Liahona*, May 2009, 87–88.
[46] Tad R. Callister, *The Infinite Atonement* (Salt Lake City: Deseret Book, 2000), 83–90.

and awakened them, seeing the torches of the approaching soldiers in the distance. As always, Jesus was ready and willing to do what lay before Him.

As we now close this chapter, which contains references to some of the most eternally significant events in Christ's life, reflect for a moment on the words of the hymn "O God, the Eternal Father," that speak reverently of the sacred ordinance instituted on that Thursday, followed by Christ's selfless, unimaginable suffering in the garden later that night.

> O God, th'Eternal Father,
> Who dwells amid the sky,
> In Jesus' name we ask thee
> To bless and sanctify,
> If we are pure before thee,
> This bread and cup of wine,
> That we may all remember
> That offering divine—
>
> That sacred, holy off'ring,
> By man least understood,
> To have our sins remitted
> And take his flesh and blood,
> That we may ever witness
> The suff'ring of thy Son,
> And always have his Spirit
> To make our hearts as one.
>
> When Jesus, the Anointed,
> Descended from above

And gave himself a ransom
To win our souls with love—
With no apparent beauty,
That man should him desire—
He was the promised Savior,
To purify with fire.

How infinite that wisdom,
The plan of holiness,
That made salvation perfect
And veiled the Lord in flesh,
To walk upon his footstool
And be like man, almost,
In his exalted station,
And die, or all was lost.[47]

Questions to Ponder

- Reflect for a moment on the two quotes mentioned in this chapter about the sacrament. President Russell M. Nelson taught, "We commemorate His Atonement in a very personal way. We bring a broken heart and a contrite spirit to our sacrament meeting. It is the highlight of our Sabbath-day observance."[48] And Elder Melvin J. Ballard declared, "I am a witness that there is a spirit attending the administration of the sacrament that warms the soul from head to foot; you feel the wounds of the spirit being healed, and the load being lifted. Comfort and happiness come to the soul that is worthy

---

47 "O God, the Eternal Father," *Hymns*, no. 175.
48 Russell M. Nelson, "Worshiping at Sacrament Meeting," *Ensign* or *Liahona*, Aug. 2004.

and truly desirous of partaking of this spiritual food."[49] What does the sacrament ordinance mean to you? How do you make that ordinance as personally significant as possible each Sunday?
- We are commanded to abide in Jesus Christ in order to receive of His strength and power and an eventual mansion in the celestial kingdom of our God. To abide means to believe in Him, to remain connected to Him, to be true to Him, and to have faith and trust in Him. How would you evaluate your ability to abide in Jesus Christ? What can you do to strengthen your resolve?
- The Lord promised He would not leave His Apostles, nor us, comfortless. This blessing is fulfilled in so many real ways through the gift of the Holy Ghost. How have you felt the strengthening, comforting, reassuring, testifying, and healing power of this third member of the Godhead?
- On the night of His great sacrifice, the Savior demonstrated the sacred and essential role of music. What role does sacred music play in your life? How can it be of even greater influence?
- Perhaps the most introspective and important question we might ask ourselves is, what does the Atonement of Jesus Christ, especially the events that transpired in the Garden of Gethsemane, mean to you? How is the power of Jesus Christ, through the Atonement, changing you and helping you to become as He is?

---

[49] Melvin J. Ballard, *Melvin J. Ballard: Crusader for Righteousness* (Salt Lake City: Bookcraft, 1966), 132–133.

Day Six
FRIDAY

CHAPTER PREVIEW

Beginning with Judas's betrayal and ending with Christ's Crucifixion and death, the events and experiences of Friday were horrendously strenuous and unspeakably exhausting and humiliating, yet they were eternally essential. On this day, Christ was betrayed by one of His closest associates; was tried for and found guilty of uncommitted acts; was wrongfully condemned to death; was scourged in a most inhumane and violent manner; was brutally nailed to a wooden cross; suffered completely alone the consequences of every sin, pain, illness, and affliction of all of humanity; and then, voluntarily and on His own terms, gave up His mortal life. Following His death, Jesus's body was carefully placed in a borrowed tomb. The word excruciating is woefully inadequate to describe the pain, agony, and feelings of utter loneliness our Lord Jesus Christ, of necessity, endured on this day for you, for me, and for each of His Father's creations.

AT SOME TIME, LATE THURSDAY night or early Friday morning, the Jewish authorities and guards, following the lead of the traitor and betrayer Judas Iscariot, encountered Jesus and His

Apostles in or near the Garden of Gethsemane. They likely first attempted to find them at the home where the Passover supper had been held.[50] Not discovering them there, Judas must have assumed Jesus would be found in the garden, since He "ofttimes resorted thither with his disciples" (John 18:2).

Approaching Jesus, Judas said, "Hail, master" (Matthew 26:49), and then, as Elder Talmage wrote, "profaned his Lord's sacred face with a kiss."[51] Unafraid, Jesus moved toward the officers and asked, "Whom seek ye?" They replied, "Jesus of Nazareth," to which our Savior responded, "I am he" (John 18:4–5). Though the agreed-upon kiss had been given, these officers were still noticeably startled or even frightened to actually be in such close proximity to the one they had been conspiring to apprehend for so long. Jesus again acknowledged His identity and asked that His Apostles be permitted to depart in safety. He was always found caring for those around Him, especially those who demonstrated acceptance of Him and His divine mission.

When Jesus was taken into custody, Peter impetuously drew a sword and smote off the ear of one of the captors. In complete emotional control, Jesus restored and healed the ear then chastised Peter, reminding him that if Jesus so desired, He could pray to the Father and twelve legions of angels would be rushed immediately to His aid (Matthew 26:53). Perhaps Peter then remembered the fate of the barren fig tree earlier in the week. If Christ so desired, He could instantly smite and destroy His captors. However, Jesus knew His time had come, and He willingly surrendered.

---

50 James E. Talmage, *Jesus the Christ* (Salt Lake City: Deseret Book Company, 1982), 614–15.
51 Ibid.

From Palm Sunday to Easter Sunday

During the night, Jesus was first taken, according to the gospel writer John, to Annas, a former Jewish high priest and father-in-law of the current high priest, Caiaphas. The reason for this first interview is unknown, though some untoward motive certainly prompted the encounter. From Annas, Jesus was then taken to the palace of Caiaphas; where the Sanhedrin, composed of chief priests, scribes, and elders, predominately of the influential Sadducee sect, was formally assembled, and under whose judgment Jesus would be tried.

What next ensued were perhaps the most unlawful, thoroughly biased, inhumane, and most hate-filled legal proceedings ever conducted in the history of the world. A short but representative list of the illegalities perpetrated during the trial follows:

- It was illegal for the Sanhedrin to convene at night, especially when considering an alleged capital offense.
- Christ was directly interrogated by Caiaphas, the high priest, and commanded to testify against Himself. Jewish law required that the judge protect the interest of the defendant and never deny him or her due process.
- No witnesses were asked to summarize their charges at the beginning of the procedure.
- When Jesus appropriately sought redress for illegal questioning, He was struck with a savage blow to the face.
- The testimony of the witnesses that were eventually found conflicted one with the other.
- Toward the end of the trial, when the charge of blasphemy was eventually settled on, Jesus was again pressed to testify against Himself when asked by Caiaphas, "I adjure thee

by the living God, that thou tell us whether thou be the Christ, the Son of God" (Matthew 26:63).[52]

Despite the inequities, injustices, and utter falsehoods that occurred and were alleged, Jesus replied to Caiaphas's interrogatory by acknowledging, "Thou hast said" (Matthew 26:64), meaning, "I am what thou hast said."[53] To this, the high priest, with the approbation of the Sanhedrin, pronounced Jesus guilty of death for blasphemy, the most serious offense in Jewish law. Ironically, as Elder Talmage explained, "Jehovah was convicted of blasphemy against Jehovah."[54]

Jewish law required a second convening of the Sanhedrin whenever one was found guilty of a capital offense in order to ensure that the accused had been properly treated, that appropriate legal procedures had been followed, and that equity and justice had been applied during the first tribunal. Though none of those requirements had been met during the initial trial, a hasty assemblage of the Sanhedrin in the early hours of the morning confirmed the guilty verdict.

While Jesus was arraigned before the Sanhedrin, Peter and perhaps others of the Apostles waited outside during the night. Mingling among other townspeople, Peter was identified three times as one who was a follower of "Jesus of Galilee" (Matthew 26:69). On each occasion, he denied his association with the Savior. On the third such denial the cock crowed, in literal fulfillment of a prophecy Jesus had given not many days before. Experiencing firsthand his own weakness, Peter went out and wept bitterly. Impetuous and,

---

52 James E. Talmage, *Jesus the Christ* (Salt Lake City: Deseret Book Company, 1982), 621–25.
53 Ibid, 626.
54 Ibid, 629.

on that night, cowardly Peter later became one of the most stalwart and fierce advocates of the Resurrected Lord, Jesus Christ, even unto death.

Roman law forbade the Jews from executing one of their own. A recommended capital punishment needed to be reviewed, approved, and carried out by the highest Roman authority in the region, who, in this case, was Pontius Pilate. So the contingent made their way to the temporary residence and judgment hall of the Roman governor of Judaea. Arriving in the early-morning hours, members of the Sanhedrin presented the Man and the charge to Pilate outside his abode. The Jews wanted to avoid becoming unclean by entering the home of a gentile—oh, the hypocrisy!

Though Jesus had been found guilty of blasphemy, the Jewish leaders accused Him in front of Pilate of sedition against Roman law and leadership, suggesting that Jesus had held Himself to be "Christ a King" (Luke 23:2). They said Jesus had been found worthy of death, and they came seeking Pilate to carry out the sentence. The Sanhedrin had no qualms substituting blasphemy, the most serious crime in Jewish law, with high treason, the most serious crime in Roman law. How convenient.

Pilate took Jesus into the judgment hall and asked Him, "Art thou the King of the Jews?" to which Jesus responded, "My kingdom is not of this world" (John 18:33, 36). After further questioning and consideration, Pilate could find no guilt in the accused. When Pilate conveyed the prisoner and communicated his judgment—in this case, acquittal—the Sanhedrin would have nothing to do with it. They argued even more vehemently. During the disagreement Pilate discovered Jesus was from Galilee, which suggested another course of action. Pilate sent Jesus to Herod, the vassal ruler of the Galilean province who happened to be in Jerusalem for the Passover.

Herod Antipas, son of Herod the Great, was he who had previously ordered the murder of John the Baptist. Though Herod was pleased to have the opportunity to meet Jesus, hoping to witness a miracle of some kind, Jesus's intentions were otherwise. Imagine how Christ must have felt standing before the man who had ordered the beheading of John, a beloved friend and the man sent to testify of and prepare the way for the one whose "shoe's latchet [he was] not worthy to unloose" (John 1:27). Regardless of the questions asked, Jesus maintained perfect composure, refusing to utter a single word. Again, Christ had the power, as demonstrated on Monday with the barren fig tree, to smite and destroy. However, He refrained. In the end, Herod sent Jesus back to Pilate, having found nothing with which to condemn Him.

Upon the return of the prisoner and the Jewish officers, Pilate reminded them that he found no fault in Jesus that would be worthy of death. Nevertheless, they continued to demand His execution. Another potential escape from this compromising situation occurred to Pilate. At the Passover season, he had the right to release a condemned prisoner. Barabbas, a convicted murderer, was being held prisoner at the time. Certainly, Pilate must have thought, the Jews would much rather release Jesus than a hardened criminal. To his surprise, however, the Jews demanded the release of Barabbas and the crucifixion of Jesus.

Pilate requested a bowl of water and washed his hands, symbolically disclaiming any responsibility for what was to happen, and said, "I am innocent of the blood of this just person: see ye to it" (Matthew 27:24). To this the Jews cried out, "His blood be on us, and on our children" (Matthew 27:25). How prophetically they spoke. Pilate released Barabbas and gave Jesus to the guards to be scourged, a common practice prior to crucifixion.

Oftentimes the one being scourged died during the very act, avoiding the further agony and awful horror of crucifixion.[55] Bound into the end of the whip used for scourging were pieces of metal and jagged fragments of bone. Silently Jesus withstood the blows. Clearly Isaiah saw in vision Christ's final hours when he wrote prophetically, "But he was wounded for our transgressions, he was bruised for our iniquities: the chastisement of our peace was upon him; and with his stripes we are healed" (Isaiah 53:5).

Weakened from scourging, Jesus then had a crown of thorns placed on His head, a purple robe draped over His shoulders, and a reed, connoting a royal scepter, placed in His hand. With the same reed, the Roman soldiers smote Jesus upon the head, driving the thorns deep into His scalp, mockingly saying, "Hail, King of the Jews!" (John 19:3).

Pause for a moment and consider the scene and implications. Jesus Christ, the Savior of *all* mankind—including those who mocked, reviled, and scourged Him, and those who demanded His death—stood as erect as His weakened frame would allow. The sins that were, in that moment, being committed against Him were the very sins, along with countless others, for which He willingly suffered the night before

---

[55] James E. Talmage, *Jesus the Christ* (Salt Lake City: Deseret Book Company, 1982), 638; David McClister, "The Scourging of Jesus," *Truth Magazine*, vol. 44, January 2000, 11–12.

in Gethsemane and would suffer later that very day, without the aid and comfort of His Father, on the cross. Ironically, not only did Christ willingly and without complaint suffer the pain of the whip, the throbbing agony of the crown of thorns, and eventually the excruciating torture of the nails driven into His hands and feet, but He also voluntarily suffered for the sinful acts that provoked this vile behavior. If any of us feel that life is simply unfair, we might consider for a moment how horribly unfair this very situation was for Christ. Yet, He endured it patiently and well, with a heart full of love for the perpetrators. Christ knew perfectly and intimately that of which He spoke during the Sermon on the Mount when He said, "Blessed are ye, when men shall revile you, and persecute you, and shall say all manner of evil against you falsely" (Matthew 5:11). No one can question our Savior's ability to live perfectly what He preached. May we seek to follow His example and rise above the injustices of mortality.

Taking Jesus out onto his balcony and hoping for one last chance to avoid meting out the punishment, Pilate presented Him to the multitude gathered outside, who, together with the scribes and priests, called vindictively for Jesus's crucifixion. Finally Pilate again capitulated and said, "Take ye him, and crucify him: for I find no fault in him" (John 19:6). Oh, the irony of that statement! In it Pilate acknowledged Christ's innocence, yet he still delivered Him up to be crucified.

Weakened from the ordeal endured during the past twelve or so hours, Jesus attempted to drag His own cross to Golgotha. Impatiently the Roman guards conscripted a Jewish man entering Jerusalem to carry the cross for Him. Slowly they made their way to the north side of the city, just outside the city walls.

From Palm Sunday to Easter Sunday

As is generally known, crucifixion was the most demoralizing and painful form of death practiced by the Romans at the time. Insufferable pain was felt initially in hands, arms, chest, and feet. Then, as fatigue increased, muscles would begin to cramp, breathing would become increasingly labored, infection and fever would develop, and thirst would become intolerable. The suffering from hanging on the cross would often last many hours or even days.[56]

At about nine o'clock Friday morning (Mark 15:25), the horrific process began.[57] With spikes driven through His hands and feet, Christ was hanged on a cross between two robbers. The Roman guards placed a plaque above Jesus's head that read, in three languages, "This is Jesus the King of the Jews" (John 19:19–20; Matthew 27:37). The sign was placed, according to custom, for the purpose of communicating to onlookers the name and offense of the condemned.[58] Though the Jewish leaders implored Pilate to alter the wording, he refused, saying, "What I have written I have written" (John 19:21–22). Pilate's rejection of their plea may have been his way of either countering the Sanhedrin's demand for the execution of one whom Pilate believed was innocent, or perhaps Pilate may have partially believed Jesus's assertion that He was a King but that His kingdom was indeed "not of this world" (John 18:36).

---

56 James E. Talmage, *Jesus the Christ* (Salt Lake City: Deseret Book Company, 1982), 655, 661; C. Truman Davis, "A Physician's View of the Crucifixion of Jesus Christ," March 29, 2018, cbn.com.

57 In the time of Christ, the Jewish people accounted for daytime hours as follows: daytime began at sunup (or about 6:00 A.M.); the "third hour," therefore, was about 9:00 A.M.; the "sixth hour" was about noon; the "ninth hour" was about 3:00 P.M.; and the end of daytime would have been at sundown, or about 6:00 P.M.

58 James E. Talmage, *Jesus the Christ* (Salt Lake City: Deseret Book Company, 1982), 656.

While on the cross the Savior spoke seven times. Only three will be noted here. The first, directed to the Roman soldiers, came as He prayed to the Father, saying, "Father, forgive them; for they know not what they do" (Luke 23:34). In a moment of great agony, there was still found a heart full of compassion for those who did not fully understand the significance of what they had been ordered to do.

Knowing the end was near and that he must attempt one last time to prevent Christ from successfully fulfilling His mortal mission, Satan persuaded the all-too-willing Jewish antagonistic leaders to begin taunting and tempting the Lord, saying, "If he be the King of Israel, let him now come down from the cross, and we will believe him." And, "He trusted in God; let him deliver him now, if he will have him: for he said, I am the Son of God" (Matthew 27:42–43). At the beginning of Jesus's earthly ministry, when the stakes were high, Satan tempted Jesus, hoping to cause Him to doubt His divine Sonship or improperly use His sacred power. Again, when the stakes were even higher, came Satan by means of ill-intended, evil-minded men, attempting to cause Jesus to stumble. Of course, Jesus remained true to His mission.

At about noon (Mark 15:33), blackness began to settle over the land. This intense darkness lasted for about three hours. Seemingly the very earth mourned the imminent death of its Creator. Then, at about three o'clock in the afternoon (Mark 15:34), a distressed, heartbroken cry was uttered by Jesus, "Eloi, Eloi, lama sabachthani? which is, being interpreted, My God, my God, why hast thou forsaken me?" (Mark 15:34). Try to picture in your mind Christ, struggling in pain, uttering those beseeching words to His Beloved Father. Words cannot describe the loneliness He must have felt.

Not only had Satan challenged his nemesis with the "if" taunts meant to elicit doubt but everything he and his minions could unleash against the Savior of the world, as had been done the night before, was unleashed as Jesus hung on the cross. The weight of the sins, pains, afflictions, illnesses—both mental and physical—and every other form of suffering that is inherently mortal and everything Satan was appropriately permitted to do, was again done at that moment of all moments. And, in the midst of it all, not only was an angel *not* sent from God to support Him (as had occurred in Gethsemane) but the sustaining Spirit of the Father was withheld momentarily from His Most Beloved Son, so that the Savior could, desperately and completely alone, finish His "preparations unto the children of men" (D&C 19:19).

Not many days earlier, Christ, who was now nigh unto death Himself, had miraculously raised his beloved friend Lazarus from the dead. That miracle, like none other, had galvanized the hatred of the Jewish priests against Jesus and strengthened their resolve to see Him killed. This cherished friend Lazarus, among other faithful followers, now almost certainly stood nearby, witnessing the final moments of his Savior's life, powerless to save Him. What Christ had done for so many during His ministry in the form of relieving suffering could not now be done for Him. He had performed countless miracles for others. However, the only miracle that could be performed on behalf of the Son of God came, not in the form of divine intervention but in the form of His Father's divine restraint, as discussed in the next paragraph.

Elder Melvin J. Ballard contemplated and then wrote how he imagined God the Father must have felt to witness His Beloved Son suffering in agony. He said:

> In that hour I think I can see our dear Father behind the veil looking upon these dying struggles until even he could not endure it any longer; . . . he bowed his head, and hid in some part of his universe, his great heart almost breaking for the love that he had for his Son. Oh, in that moment when he might have saved his Son, I thank him and praise him that he did not fail us, for he had not only the love of his Son in mind, but he also had love for us. I rejoice that he did not interfere, and that his love for us made it possible for him to endure . . . the sufferings of his Son and give him finally to us, our Savior and our Redeemer.[59]

When the requisite suffering had been completed, His Father's Spirit returned, the hopeless feeling of being forsaken departed, and Jesus knew this eternally essential part of His mission was complete. In a spirit of humble triumph, the Savior of Mankind, mustering as much strength as He could, likely raised His head heavenward when He announced, "It is finished" (John 19:30). Reverently addressing Elohim, Jesus said, "Father, into thy hands I commend my spirit" (Luke 23:46). Can you feel the deep love this perfect Son had for His Father? With that, Jesus respectfully bowed His head and voluntarily gave up His mortal life.

At the death of Jesus, two important events transpired. First, a tremendous earthquake violently shook the earth, similar to what occurred on the American continent. This

---

59 Bryant S. Hinckley, *Sermons and Missionary Services of Melvin Joseph Ballard* (Salt Lake City: Deseret Book Company, 1949), 147–57.

caused a Roman centurion to proclaim, "Certainly this was a righteous man" (Luke 23:47) and others to affirm, "Truly this was the Son of God" (Matthew 27:54). Even the earth itself, one of Christ's creations, seemed to testify of its divine Creator and groan at His passing. Second, in the midst of the earthquake, the veil of the temple that hung between the Holy Place and the Holy of Holies was rent completely, signifying, according to Elder Talmage, "the rending of Judaism, the consummation of the Mosaic dispensation, and the inauguration of Christianity under apostolic administration."[60]

The Jewish Sabbath would begin with the setting of the sun (at about 6:00 P.M.), and it was already late in the afternoon. Fearful of desecrating the Sabbath by leaving men hanging on the cross on that sacred day (again, the hypocrisy is without equal), the Jewish authorities obtained Pilate's permission to break the men's legs, a practice that normally would bring about instantaneous death. The deed, in fact, did cause the robbers to shudder and succumb, but when the Jewish leaders discovered that Jesus was already dead, they withheld, preserving the perfect analogy between Him and the paschal lamb that must be one without blemish or broken bone (Exodus 12:46; Psalm 34:20). A Roman soldier, to verify Christ's death, thrust a sword into His side, leaving a wound that His disciples both in Jerusalem and in the New World would later witness.

A wealthy disciple of Christ, known as Joseph of Arimathæa, sought and secured permission of Pilate to give Jesus's body a proper burial. Assisted by Nicodemus, who had months earlier been taught the need for spiritual rebirth (John 3:3–5), Joseph wrapped the body in cloth, "with . . . spices, as the manner of the Jews is to bury" (John 19:40), and laid it

---

60 James E. Talmage, *Jesus the Christ* (Salt Lake City: Deseret Book Company, 1982), 662.

in his own unused sepulcher. Some devoted women watched the burial a short distance off to verify its location and ensure its proper completion then returned home to observe the Sabbath (Matthew 27:61; Mark 15:47; Luke 23:55).

The first five verses of the hymn "Behold the Great Redeemer Die," capture in majestic detail both the events and the spirit of this agonizing day:

> Behold the great Redeemer die,
> A broken law to satisfy.
> He dies a sacrifice for sin,
> He dies a sacrifice for sin,
> That man may live and glory win.
>
> While guilty men his pains deride,
> They pierce his hands and feet and side;
> And with insulting scoffs and scorns,
> And with insulting scoffs and scorns,
> They crown his head with plaited thorns.
>
> Although in agony he hung,
> No murm'ring word escaped his tongue.
> His high commission to fulfill,
> His high commission to fulfill,
> He magnified his Father's will.
>
> "Father, from me remove this cup.
> Yet, if thou wilt, I'll drink it up.
> I've done the work thou gavest me;
> I've done the work thou gavest me;
> Receive my spirit unto thee."

> He died, and at the awful sight
> The sun in shame withdrew its light!
> Earth trembled, and all nature sighed,
> Earth trembled, and all nature sighed,
> In dread response, "A God has died!"[61]

Nearly thirty-four years before this day's events, Mary conceived then nine months later gave mortal life to the literal Son of the very Eternal Father. There were three principle reasons God the Father needed to be Jesus Christ's literal Father: so that Jesus would have the power to withstand the onslaught that would transpire in Gethsemane and on Calvary without prematurely perishing, to voluntarily give up His own life at a time when His own mortal mission had been completely fulfilled, and to take His body back up again through the ordinance of Resurrection. Two of the three reasons for Christ's Divine Sonship were complete. Only one remained.

Questions to Ponder
- What feelings enter your heart as you consider the illegal, inhumane, completely biased, and hate-filled treatment Jesus received at the hands of the Jewish Sanhedrin?
- How do you feel as you consider that Jesus willingly permitted this evil treatment and spoke not a single spiteful word?
- What additional thoughts or feelings do you have as you contemplate your Savior, hanging completely alone on the cross, suffering beyond everything imaginable, until the uttermost price was paid, in perfect fulfillment of His premortal commitment?

---
61 "Behold the Great Redeemer Die," *Hymns*, no. 191.

Day Seven
SATURDAY

CHAPTER PREVIEW

On Saturday, while His body lay peacefully in the tomb whose entrance was heavily guarded by Roman soldiers, Christ's eternal Spirit went, in fulfillment of His premortal promise, to the world of the spirits. There He declared the day of salvation to believers and organized and initiated the preaching of His gospel to unbelievers. The commitment He made in the great Council in Heaven, long before this world was created, was perfectly fulfilled. It is important to understand that much of what occurred during Christ's final week on Earth is generally accepted by the Christian world; however, the reality of the spirit world and Christ's ministry to the spirits who awaited there are two verities that were clouded by the effects of the Apostasy and required latter-day revelation to reestablish their truthfulness. Understanding of the eternally significant events of that Saturday was restored and seen in glorious vision by President Joseph F. Smith the night before general conference in October of 1918, and it is recounted in this chapter.

THOUGH THEY HAD SEEMINGLY SUCCEEDED in removing Jesus Christ as an impediment to their dogmatic ways, the chief priests and Pharisees awoke on the Sabbath with a significant concern. They recalled that Jesus had said while still alive, "After three days I will rise again" (Matthew 27:63). While they did not believe this would actually occur, they feared that Christ's disciples would remove His body from the tomb and claim He had risen. These rulers quickly approached Pilate and requested permission to seal the tomb and place guards to prevent anyone from disturbing Jesus's burial place. Little did they know that there was no seal strong enough nor army great enough to prevent what would happen the following day. While those guards stood watch, Jesus, in Spirit, continued His great work, fulfilling the will of His Father.

In the New Testament book of 1 Peter, chapter 3, verses 18–20, we read the following:

> For Christ also hath once suffered for sins, the just for the unjust, that he might bring us to God, being put to death in the flesh, but quickened by the Spirit: By which also he went and preached unto the spirits in prison; Which sometime were disobedient, when once the longsuffering of God waited in the days of Noah, while the ark was a preparing, wherein few, that is, eight souls were saved by water.

Related doctrine is taught in 1 Peter 4:6, which reads, "for this cause was the gospel preached also to them that are dead, that they might be judged according to men in the flesh, but live according to God in the spirit."

The belief that Christ "preached unto the spirits in prison" while His body lay in the tomb was common among

Christians for the first few centuries following His Ascension. However, as was the case with so many other doctrines; the darkening, deceiving, and distorting effects of the Apostasy gradually crept in and caused what seemed clear and obvious to become clouded, misunderstood, and even forgotten. To appreciate the reality of Christ's activities on that Saturday, a brief review is necessary of the existence, subsequent loss, and then eventual restoration of the doctrine of the spirit world and Christ's ministry to the dead.

The following are statements by some of the early Christian fathers who lived during the first two centuries A.D. that corroborate the doctrine taught in 1 Peter about the reality of a spirit world and that Christ personally shared His gospel among those who awaited the Resurrection there.

Irenaeus, a Greek Christian cleric born in 130 A.D., preached openly of the spirit world as follows: ". . . it is manifest that the souls of [Christ's] disciples . . . shall go away into the invisible place allotted to them by God, and there remain until the resurrection, awaiting that event."[62]

Justin Martyr, a Christian philosopher who was born in 100 A.D. and martyred in 165 A.D., also taught the reality of the spirit world, in addition to the division of spirits there, when he said, "The souls of the pious remain in a better place, while those of the unjust and wicked are in a worse, waiting for the time of judgment."[63]

Origen, an early Christian scholar, theologian, and prolific writer, was born in Alexandria, Egypt, in about 184 A.D.

---

62 Irenaeus, *Against Heresies* 5:31, in Roberts, Alexander, and James Donaldson, eds. *The Ante-Nicene Fathers*, 1:560–561, Buffalo: The Christian Literature Publishing Company, 1885–1896.

63 Justin Martyr, *Dialogue with Trypho 5*, in Roberts, Alexander, and James Donaldson, eds. *The Ante-Nicene Fathers*, 1:197, Buffalo: The Christian Literature Publishing Company, 1885–1896; cf. Davies, *The Early Christian Church*, 100.

and not only taught of the spirit world but also that those who dwell there will receive instruction. He stated,

> I think . . . that all the saints who depart from this life will remain in some place situated on the earth, which holy Scripture calls paradise, as in some place of instruction, and, so to speak, class-room or school of souls, in which they are to be instructed regarding all the things which they had seen on earth, and are to receive also some information respecting things that are to follow in the future.[64]

We continue to increase our understanding of these anciently understood principles by reference to *The Gospel of Nicodemus*, an apocryphal gospel believed by some to have resulted from an original Hebrew work written by Nicodemus, a disciple of Christ. There we read as follows of the coming of the "King of glory," Jesus Christ, to set free "all the dead who had been bound" and that "the angels of the Lord say: The Lord strong and mighty, the Lord mighty in battle. And immediately with these words the brazen gates were shattered, and the iron bars broken, and all the dead who had been bound came out of the prisons. . . . And the King of glory came in in the form of a man, and all the dark places . . . were lighted up."[65] While *The Gospel of Nicodemus*

---

[64] Origen, *De Principiis* 2:11:6, in Roberts, Alexander, and James Donaldson, eds. *The Ante-Nicene Fathers*, 4:299, Buffalo: The Christian Literature Publishing Company, 1885-1896.

[65] *The Gospel of Nicodemus*, in Roberts, Alexander, and James Donaldson, eds. *The Ante-Nicene Fathers*, 8:438, Buffalo: The Christian Literature Publishing Company, 1885–1896.

is not included in our canon of holy scripture, it sheds interesting and even confirmatory light on the activities of Christ during that fateful Saturday.

Finally, here are two quotes that speak further about Christ's personal ministry and His preaching of the gospel among the spirits. Origen, referenced earlier, said, "When He [Jesus Christ] became a soul, without the covering of the body, He dwelt among those souls which were without bodily covering, converting such of them as were willing to Himself."[66] Again quoting Justin Martyr, we read, "The Lord God remembered His dead people of Israel who lay in the graves; and He descended to preach to them His own salvation."[67]

Despite the clarity of the doctrine taught in 1 Peter and the statements we have just reviewed, made by many of the early Christian fathers regarding the reality of a spirit world and Christ's ministry in that world on that Saturday following His crucifixion, the Apostasy that spread across the world during the centuries preceding Joseph Smith clouded those views. Such darkness caused Christians in the days of the Prophet Joseph Smith, and yet today, to believe in a confusing variety of postmortal concepts. Some believe the spirit enters a state of unconsciousness while awaiting the Resurrection. Others believe the spirit receives its eternal reward immediately (heaven, hell, or an intermediate place for further cleansing called purgatory), though the Final Judgment and Resurrection occur later, when Christ comes in glory. Still others believe death is a state of nonexistence

---

66 Origen, *Against Celsus* 2:43, in Roberts, Alexander, and James Donaldson, eds. *The Ante-Nicene Fathers*, 4:448, Buffalo: The Christian Literature Publishing Company, 1885–1896.

67 Justin Martyr, *Dialogue with Trypho* 71–72, in Roberts, Alexander, and James Donaldson, eds. *The Ante-Nicene Fathers*, 1:234–235, Buffalo: The Christian Literature Publishing Company, 1885–1896.

for the soul until the Resurrection. Finally, others, while they believe in the continuation of the spirit, do not believe in the reality of the Resurrection. Few teach much of anything of Christ's ministry among the spirits on that Saturday while his body lay in the tomb.[68]

However, with the glory of the Restoration that began to enlighten the world, knowledge that had been lost commenced to pour down from heaven upon the hearts and minds of God's prophets. One of those prophets who played a very significant role in restoring knowledge regarding Christ's activities during the time His body lay in the sepulcher was President Joseph F. Smith, the sixth prophet of the Restoration.

On the night of October 3, 1918, the day before a general conference of the Church, President Smith sat in his room pondering the scriptures referenced above from 1 Peter. What came clearly that night was a pearl of precious truth explaining Jesus's undertakings during the time His body lay in the tomb and how the gospel of Christ was preached in the spirit world to both those who were just and dwelled in paradise and those who dwelled in prison. Reviewing portions of that vision President Smith received and that was later included in our canon of holy scripture is

---

68 "Afterlife and Salvation," Patheos, http://www.patheos.com/library/protestantism/beliefs/afterlife-and-salvation; "Eternal Life (Christianity)," Wikipedia, April 6, 2018, https://en.wikipedia.org/wiki/Eternal_life_(Christianity); "What Happens to Our Bodies Immediately after We Die?" Jim Blackburn, Catholic Answers, August 4, 2011, https://www.catholic.com/qa/what-happens-to-our-bodies-immediately-after-we-die; "Purgatory," Catholic Answers, August 10, 2004, https://www.catholic.com/tract/purgatory; "Christian Views on Life after Death," GCSE Religious Studies at HGS, https://hgsrs.wordpress.com/about/immortality/christian-views-on-life-after-death/.

perhaps the most appropriate and effective way to explain the events that occurred in Jesus's life on that Saturday.

President Smith spoke of the vision as it burst forth upon him, saying, "As I pondered over these things which are written [1 Peter 3:18–20; 4:6], the eyes of my understanding were opened, and the Spirit of the Lord rested upon me, and I saw the hosts of the dead, both small and great" (D&C 138:11). Referencing the delight felt by the awaiting righteous spirits because of Christ's imminent visit, President Smith said, "I beheld that they were filled with joy and gladness, and were rejoicing together because the day of their deliverance was at hand" (D&C 138:15). Imagine being one of those spirits who had waited millennia to be set free and receive the blessing and glory of the holy Resurrection!

The record of President Smith's supernal vision continues: "While this vast multitude waited and conversed, rejoicing in the hour of their deliverance from the chains of death, the Son of God appeared, declaring liberty to the captives who had been faithful; and there he preached to them the everlasting gospel, the doctrine of the resurrection and the redemption of mankind from the fall, and from individual sins on conditions of repentance" (D&C 138:18–19). Oh, the joy, gladness, warmth, and peace they must have felt when their Redeemer appeared, declaring liberty to the righteous captives! I think of the personal ministry that occurred by Jesus among His disciples in the Americas, where they bore witness of Him, were blessed by Him, heard Him pray for them, and were taught His everlasting gospel. This occasion in the spirit world must have been similarly stirring and rewarding.

However, the question must be asked, but what of the wicked, those who openly rejected Him in mortality? Did Christ minister unto them as well? The answer came in the following three verses: "But unto the wicked he did not go, and among the ungodly and the unrepentant who had defiled themselves while in the flesh, his voice was not raised; Neither did the rebellious who rejected the testimonies and the warnings of the ancient prophets behold his presence, nor look upon his face. Where these were, darkness reigned, but among the righteous there was peace" (D&C 138:20–22).

At this point, President Smith wondered about these unrighteous spirits in prison and how the seemingly innumerable hosts there would receive His gospel and have an appropriate opportunity to progress, according to their spiritual readiness and willingness. As he pondered, the record states, "my eyes were opened, and my understanding quickened, and I perceived that the Lord went not in person among the wicked and the disobedient who had rejected the truth, to teach them; but behold, from among the righteous, he organized his forces and appointed messengers, clothed with power and authority, and commissioned them to go forth and carry the light of the gospel to them that were in darkness, even to all the spirits of men; and thus was the gospel preached to the dead" (D&C 138:29–30).

Christ clearly understood, as beautifully clarified for us through the lens of modern revelation to living prophets, that His mission was to provide the means whereby *all* of God's children would have the opportunity to return to the presence of the Father, not just those among whom He had ministered on Earth. This mission carried into the spirit world, where His gospel was preached to the just and the unjust, to some through His own personal ministry and to others through the ministry of ordained servants. Confirming the all-encompassing nature of Christ's mission, the Prophet Joseph Smith declared that "all those who have not had an opportunity of hearing the Gospel, and being administered unto by an inspired man in the flesh, must have it hereafter, before they can be finally judged."[69] In fulfillment of that eternal requirement, our Savior Jesus Christ ensured that all aspects of His divine mission were fulfilled, benefitting the living and the dead.

From the beginning of time, when His gospel in its fulness has been upon the earth, God has commanded His children to build temples in which sacred, essential, saving ordinances for the worthy living could be performed. The greatest of these ordinances provides the recipient a promise of eternal life, in families, through faithfulness to His commandments. With the proclamation of the gospel by the Savior to the dead as discussed in this chapter and the Resurrection that will be addressed in the next chapter, temple ordinances could thenceforth be administered on behalf of all of God's children, living *and* dead. This glorious doctrine, not understood by the world at large, explains the necessity of latter-day temples and the majesty of the work performed therein, made possible, in part, by the work Jesus performed in the spirit world that Saturday while His mortal body lay in the tomb. In the words of the hymn "Holy Temples on Mount Zion," we rejoice in the knowledge that because "the prisoners [went] free," "our faithful kindred" can be "sealed with us eternally."

---

[69] *Teaching of Presidents of the Church: Joseph Smith* [2011], 471.

Holy temples on Mount Zion
In a lofty splendor shine,
Avenues to exaltation,
Symbols of a love divine.
And their kindly portals beckon
To serenity and prayer,
Valiant children of the promise,
Pledged to sacred service there.

Merciful and gracious Father,
Purify our hearts, we pray;
Bless our mission of redemption
In thy hallowed house each day,
Till at length our faithful kindred,
Sealed with us eternally
In celestial bonds of union,
Sing hosannas unto thee.

Sing aloud, ye heav'nly chorus,
Anthems of eternal praise
To the glorious King Immanuel!
Sing with Saints of latter days!
Let the mountains shout for gladness,
And the valleys joyful be,
While the stars acclaim in rapture,
For the prisoners shall go free.[70]

Question to Ponder
- What thoughts come to mind as you ponder the perfection and all-inclusiveness of God's plan for His

---

[70] "Holy Temples on Mount Zion" by Archibald F. Bennett/Alexander Schreiner © by Intellectual Reserve, Inc., *Hymns*, no. 289.

children and His determination that Christ's saving power and grace be made available to everyone, both living and dead?

Day Eight
EASTER SUNDAY

CHAPTER PREVIEW

While we do not know precisely the hour our Savior was resurrected, we do know that it was still dark, in the early-morning hours of that Sunday, when the earth began to quake and an angel from the presence of God came down and rolled back the stone door to the tomb. Whether Christ came forth at that time or whether His Resurrection had already occurred does not matter. What does matter is that on that first Easter Sunday, after His body had lain for all or part of three days in a borrowed tomb, Jesus Christ became "the firstfruits of them that slept" (1 Corinthians 15:20), further fulfilling the requirements He had accepted in the premortal world. With this act, combined with His suffering in Gethsemane and on Calvary, all men and women who have ever or will ever experience mortality will be resurrected as an unconditional gift and be given the opportunity to return to the presence of the Father through faith on His Beloved Son, obedience to His commandments, and sincere repentance of their sins. On that day, several were witness to this glorious miracle called resurrection.

As the earliest rays of sunshine appeared over the hills to the east of Jerusalem, Mary Magdalene and other devoted women (Mark 16:1; Luke 24:10) made their way to the north side of the city where it is believed Jesus's tomb was situated. They bore ointments and spices to be used to further anoint and embalm the body of Jesus, to pay respect to their Lord and Master in the most tangible way they could. On the way they wondered how they would roll back the stone door (Mark 16:3). Nevertheless, they proceeded with faith. When they arrived they discovered that their first problem was solved: the door to the tomb was open. However, a second problem became apparent: Jesus's body was missing. The account by John suggests that Mary ran first to bear the sad news to the Apostles while the other women remained (John 20:1–2). Momentarily an angel appeared and assuaged their concerns by announcing, "He is not here: for he is risen" (Matthew 28:6). They were instructed by the angel to go and tell the Savior's disciples that He had risen from the dead and would meet them in Galilee. Imagine the combined feelings of confusion yet overwhelming joy these women must have felt, confusion because no one had ever been resurrected and they did not know precisely what that meant and joy because the announcement from the heavenly messenger suggested that their Savior and Redeemer—indeed, their dearest Friend—was alive![71]

Mary Magdalene, who, as was mentioned, may not have heard the angelic declaration, reached Peter first and said, "They have taken away the Lord . . . , and we know not where they have laid him" (John 20:2). Either, as John's

---

[71] See also Luke 24:9–11 and James E. Talmage, *Jesus the Christ* (Salt Lake City: Deseret Book, 1982), 679, 682–683.

record intimates, she was not present when the angel declared Christ's Resurrection, or she had not yet fully understood or appreciated the full extent of the term *resurrection*. It had never happened before. There was no point of comparison. She was understandably perplexed and saddened.

Peter and John ran to the tomb and, as testified, found it empty. Mary arrived shortly thereafter. Perhaps feeling there was nothing more to do, Peter and John departed. Mary, still grief-stricken, gazed again into the empty sepulcher, trying desperately to make sense of what she had seen and heard, and, more importantly, what she still felt.[72] She saw two angels sitting where Jesus's body had lain. They asked, "Woman, why weepest thou?" She tearfully replied, "They have taken away my Lord" (John 20:13).

Turning back from the tomb, Mary heard another voice ask similarly, "Woman, why weepest thou? whom seekest thou?" Thinking the question came from the gardener, she did not yet recognize the Savior and implored, "Sir, if thou have borne him hence, tell me where thou hast laid him, and I will take him away" (John 20:15). The reply came from a familiar voice that lifted her soul to the heavens: "Mary" (John 20:16). Rushing to embrace Him, Mary was forbidden because the Lord had not yet "ascended to [His] Father" (John 20:17).

A beloved woman, a daughter of God, was the first to witness the resurrected Lord. The next to see Him were other faithful women, those who had been with Mary earlier that morning at the tomb (Matthew 28:9). He commanded that they tell the Apostles to go to Galilee, where they would meet their risen Lord.

---

[72] James E. Talmage, *Jesus the Christ* (Salt Lake City: Deseret Book, 1982), 679.

While the Apostles planned to make their way to Galilee the following day, the Sanhedrin convened urgently to discuss a most perplexing problem. The Roman guards, who had been placed to secure the tomb and who had been eyewitnesses to the angel rolling back the massive stone door, reported the occurrence to the Jewish elders. In counsel, the Sanhedrin conspired to refute any accounts of a risen Jesus Christ and paid a handsome sum of money to the guards to testify that the disciples had come by night while the guards slept and had stolen the body. Normally sleeping on duty would have resulted in death to the guards, but the Jewish priests promised them protection from Pilate.

To a remorseful and deeply penitent Peter, appeared the risen Lord. The moment must have been a cherished and tender one. Peter had certainly suffered dearly for denying association with the Master. One must believe that Jesus, on such an occasion, spoke no words of reprimand, but reassured Peter warmly and affectionately.

During the afternoon of that Easter Sunday, two of Jesus's disciples were traveling to Emmaus, a village believed to have been about seven or eight miles to the west of Jerusalem. While they walked, a man joined them and engaged in conversation. The topic of greatest interest at that time was Jesus Christ and His Crucifixion. As they walked and talked, this stranger expounded the scriptures in a way that confirmed the divinity of Jesus Christ.

Reaching their destination, the three tarried longer while the stranger broke bread and blessed it. Of a sudden "their eyes were opened, and they knew him; and he vanished out of their sight" (Luke 24:31). Immediately they acknowledged

From Palm Sunday to Easter Sunday 97

among themselves, "Did not our heart burn within us, while he talked with us by the way, and while he opened to us the scriptures?" (Luke 24:32). Promptly they set out for Jerusalem to share the good news with the Apostles.

Later that night, in Jerusalem, after the two had arrived from Emmaus and shared their thrilling news, ten of the Apostles and other believers were also blessed with a sacred visit from the resurrected Lord. He appeared and said, setting their hearts at ease, "Peace be unto you" (John 20:19). Sensing their continued feelings of apprehension, Jesus further spoke, "Why are ye troubled? and why do thoughts arise in your hearts? Behold my hands and my feet, that it is I myself: handle me, and see; for a spirit hath not flesh and bones, as ye see me have" (Luke 24:38–39). Despite multiple firsthand experiences that day with the risen Lord and several of those gathered, the reality of Resurrection was still difficult for them to grasp.

Shortly thereafter Christ spoke the following words, summarizing beautifully His completed mortal mission and announcing the Apostles' forthcoming work: "Thus it is written, and thus it behoved Christ to suffer, and to rise from the dead the third day: and that repentance and remission of sins should be preached in his name among all nations, beginning at Jerusalem" (Luke 24:46–47). To support them in that sacred mission and in their individual lives, the Savior "breathed on them, and saith unto them, Receive ye the Holy Ghost" (John 20:22).

And so it was, as that first Easter Sunday came to an end, the mortal ministry and mission of Christ were fulfilled. The most momentous and eternally far-reaching responsibilities

He had received from His Father and promised to fulfill while on Earth were accomplished. "Death is conquered; man is free. Christ has won the victory."[73] Elder Neal A. Maxwell spoke fittingly when he said, "Never has anyone offered so much to so many in so few words as when Jesus said, 'Here am I, send me.'"[74]

In the April 2000 general conference, President Russell M. Nelson referred to a non-scriptural Egyptian manuscript, which recounts an intriguing interaction between the Father and the Son. This heartfelt conversation accentuates the love that was present between Father and His "beloved Son" and that was likewise expressed by the Son for all of the Father's children, when that Son volunteered to "go down to the world" and atone. The manuscript reads as follows:

> He (the Father) took the clay from the hand of the angel, and made Adam according to Our image and likeness, and He left him lying for forty days and forty nights without putting breath into him. And He heaved sighs over him daily, saying, 'If I put breath into this [man], he must suffer many pains.' And I said unto My Father, 'Put breath into him; I will be an advocate for him.' And My Father said unto Me, 'If I put breath into him, My beloved Son, Thou wilt be obliged to go down into the world, and to suffer many pains for him before Thou shalt have redeemed him, and made him to come

---

[73] "He Is Risen!" *Hymns*, no. 199.
[74] Neal A. Maxwell, "Jesus of Nazareth, Savior and King," *Ensign*, May 1976.

> back to his primal state.' And I said unto My Father, 'Put breath into him; I will be his advocate, and I will go down into the world, and will fulfil Thy command.'[75]

Though this record is non-scriptural, it captures beautifully the love our Savior felt for us in the premortal world when He agreed to come down and fulfill the Father's will. While knowing His commitment would result in suffering "many pains," Christ willingly did so because of His infinite love.

As you have read this book, my deepest hope is that you have personally felt some of that love He has for you.

So, what of this Jesus Christ? Who is He for you? In the Book of Mormon Christ spoke beautifully, compassionately, and metaphorically when He said, "I have graven thee upon the palms of my hands" (1 Nephi 21:16). Contemplate the imagery. Two days previously, on Friday, spikes were driven cruelly into His hands, the marks which now witness powerfully of His eternal love for you and all mankind. Doubtless He has "graven *thee* upon the palms of [His] hands." It is impossible for Him to forget you. He never has. He never will. The question now becomes, what role does He play in your life? And will *you* "always remember him" (Moroni 4:3)?

As the last days progress, the need to place Jesus Christ at the very center of one's life is becoming increasingly paramount. Is it any wonder that Nephi, who understood our day so well, spoke of the all-encompassing place our Savior occupied in the lives of the Nephites and should occupy in ours, by saying,

---

75 Russell M. Nelson, "The Creation," *Ensign*, May 2000.

"And we talk of Christ, we rejoice in Christ, we preach of Christ, we prophesy of Christ, and we write according to our prophecies, that our children may know to what source they may look for a remission of their sins" (2 Nephi 25:26)?

Soon Christ will come again. How we look forward—if prepared—with hearts filled with joyous anticipation, to that glorious day. In 1859 Charles W. Penrose wrote in the *Millennial Star* his description of the Savior's ominous yet ultimately glorious Second Coming as follows:

> He comes! The earth shakes, and the tall mountains tremble; the mighty deep rolls back to the north as in fear, and the rent skies glow like molten brass.
>
> He comes! The dead Saints burst forth from their tombs, and 'those who are alive and remain' are 'caught up' with them to meet him. The ungodly rush to hide themselves from his presence, and call upon the quivering rocks to cover them.
>
> He comes! with all the hosts of the righteous glorified. The breath of his lips strikes death to the wicked. His glory is a consuming fire. The proud and rebellious are as stubble; they are burned and 'left neither root nor branch.'
>
> He sweeps the earth 'as with the besom of destruction.' He deluges the earth with the fiery floods of his wrath, and the filthiness and abominations of the world are consumed.

> Satan and his dark hosts are taken and bound—the prince of the power of the air has lost his dominion, for He whose right it is to reign has come, and 'the kingdoms of this world have become the kingdoms of our Lord and of his Christ.'[76]

But must we await that prophesied day to receive Him? Does His power, through His Atonement, apply to us now or only after He comes again or in the day of the Final Judgment?

The answer is obvious. He suffered for our sins so that we can be forgiven *now* if we will humbly and sincerely repent. He experienced and suffered all the pains, afflictions, and infirmities inherent in mortality so He would know "according to the flesh how to succor his people according to their infirmities" *now* (Alma 7:12), not in some distant future day. He arose on the third day so that we can receive *now* the hope of immortality that only He can give and to know *now* and forever that the grasp of death has been broken. The promise Helaman made to his sons, Nephi and Lehi, as a guarantee to those who center their lives in Christ, applies to us *now* as much as it applied to them then. He said,

> And now, my sons, remember, remember that it is upon the rock of our Redeemer, who is Christ, the Son of God, that ye must build your foundation; that when the devil shall send forth his mighty winds, yea, his shafts in the whirlwind, yea, when all his

---

[76] Charles W. Penrose, "The Lord's Second Coming," in *Doctrines of the Gospel Student Manual* (2000), 583.

> hail and his mighty storm shall beat upon you, it shall have no power over you to drag you down to the gulf of misery and endless wo, because of the rock upon which ye are built, which is a sure foundation, a foundation whereon if men build they cannot fall. (Helaman 5:12)

Note that if we build our foundation on Him, the rock of our Redeemer, we cannot fall. Helaman did not say that we *likely will not fall or perhaps may not fall, if we are lucky*, but rather that we cannot fall. Oh, the certainty of that promise! And that promise applies to us *now*.

How does one build his foundation on Christ? It may be as simple as suggested in a single verse from King Benjamin's address:

> For the natural man is an enemy to God, and has been from the fall of Adam, and will be, forever and ever, unless he *yields to the enticings of the Holy Spirit*, and putteth off the natural man and *becometh a saint through the atonement of Christ the Lord, and becometh as a child, submissive, meek, humble, patient, full of love, willing to submit to all things which the Lord seeth fit to inflict upon him*, even as a child doth submit to his father. (Mosiah 3:19; emphases added)

Know that He is. Know that His grace is sufficient for you, no matter where you are along life's spiritual journey. Know that His promises are real. Know that He did all He said He would do. Trust in Him. Yield to Him. Humble yourself before Him. Allow your heart to be filled with His love. Now, "Come unto him" (2 Nephi 26:33). His "yoke is easy, and [His] burden is light" (Matthew 11:30). Know that you can come unto Him because He suffered, died, and LIVES.

The words penned by President Gordon B. Hinckley in the hymn "My Redeemer Lives" are a fitting conclusion to this tribute to Christ's final days on Earth and to His glorious Resurrection. They speak exultantly of the risen Lord and of the hope, faith, and peace that come from Him alone to all who follow Him.

> I know that my Redeemer lives,
> Triumphant Savior, Son of God,
> Victorious over pain and death,
> My King, my Leader, and my Lord.
>
> He lives, my one sure rock of faith,
> The one bright hope of men on earth,
> The beacon to a better way,
> The light beyond the veil of death.
>
> Oh, give me thy sweet Spirit still,
> The peace that comes alone from thee,
> The faith to walk the lonely road
> That leads to thine eternity.[77]

---

[77] "My Redeemer Lives" by Gordon B. Hinckley/G. Homer Durham © by Intellectual Reserve, Inc. *Hymns*, no. 135.

Questions to Ponder

- Imagine that you stood at the empty tomb when the angel declared, "He is not here: for he is risen" (Matthew 28:6). What would you have felt? What do you feel now as you contemplate the reality of immortality for all through the Resurrection of Jesus Christ?
- Have you felt your "heart burn within [you]" (Luke 24:32) that Jesus is the Christ and that He lives? What does that witness imply? If you have not yet felt that confirming witness, believe, ask the Father in faith, and it will come.
- As you now consider in retrospect the events of Christ's final days in mortality and His glorious Resurrection, from Palm Sunday to Easter Sunday, what do you feel about Him? Do you feel an increased closeness to Him? Are your feelings even more tender now as you consider all He experienced and has done for you?

Epilogue

When our children were younger and living at home, there were several bedtime practices we used to help them learn the gospel and feel the Spirit. First, almost every night we would gather for family scripture study and prayer. As many parents know, this pattern helps plant children in gospel soil like almost none other. While no practice is failsafe, because of agency, establishing that spiritual foundation will, sooner or later, bear righteous fruit.

Another bedtime custom was to sit on the floor at the side of each young child's bed as they were falling asleep and sing peaceful hymns or songs. My favorites were "Silent Night" and "O Come All Ye Faithful," regardless of the season. There is something about good music that calms a soul after a busy and, at times, stressful day and brings the Spirit into a child's heart.

A third nightly occurrence was part of our youngest daughter's life during several of her adolescent years. She was a voracious reader and loved novels. As she fell asleep each night, I would often sit on the floor near her bed, with a flashlight in hand, and read a few pages from Elder Gerald

N. Lund's *The Work and the Glory* series. Over the course of several years, reading a few pages each night, we made it through seven volumes and into the eighth before our schedules changed and that nearly nightly experience ended. That was a sad day for me because of the closeness developed with my daughter during those years and the sweetness of the Spirit we often felt as we read about the early latter-day saints. The practice provided natural, periodic opportunities to bear testimony of Joseph Smith, the latter-day prophet of this dispensation—testimonies that were often punctuated by tenderness and tears.

A fourth bedtime practice took the form of creative storytelling. The stories I would share were all based on fact, but in each of them I would insert an additional character, the child who was falling asleep in the bed next to me as I sat on the floor. For example, if I was telling the story of the First Vision, the story would proceed according to history, but I would place my child in the story as a silent observer, perhaps crouched behind a tree in the grove, watching and feeling that sacred occurrence.

So, why do I share these personal family experiences with you? It certainly is not to suggest that everyone should do these precise things or that my wife and I are any better parents than others who strive to instill gospel principles in their children. I am very aware that that is not the case. While we have tried to be obedient to counsel received from latter-day prophets and promptings from the Spirit, parenthood is one of the most trying, challenging, heartrending experiences of mortality, and there is certainly no room for pride in the endeavor.

The reason I share these experiences, especially the last one, is to compare that method and the desired outcome to the desired outcome of this book. As mentioned in the Preface, my hope in making this book available is to provide the means, in a simple and short yet powerful way, of helping God's children draw closer to His Son, Jesus Christ. As you read and envisioned those things Christ experienced during His final days in mortality and on through His glorious Resurrection, I hope the content allowed you to see in your mind's eye, feel in your heart, or experience as if you were there (like my children in the bedtime stories), some of the agony, the pain, the anguish, the sadness, the love, the reverence, the joy, and the ultimate triumph He felt.

My wish is that every person who reads this book and continues conscientiously on the path of discipleship will feel something more tender each time a sacrament hymn is sung, a sacrament prayer is offered, or Jesus Christ's name and mission are mentioned because they were silent observers there. I further hope the questions at the end of each chapter help provide moments of quiet introspection in order to connect the events of those final days in Christ's life to your own life and evaluate your readiness to meet Him when He comes again.

In order for such feelings to be sustained, I have found that an attitude of diligent yearning and seeking is needed. A single or even frequent reading of a book can help, especially when the content is inherently and intimately Christ-focused; but when the experience has been obtained and the heart at least temporarily changed, the question becomes, "Now what?"

A few months after completing this book, I was not feeling the same concentrated spiritual power as I did in the days and weeks immediately following that Easter Sunday. Obviously, studying and writing for three to six hours a day, in an intensely Christ-focused manner, will naturally produce generous fruits of the Spirit. While I have studied and prayed daily for decades, I experienced something from Palm Sunday to Easter Sunday in 2017 and a few weeks beyond that I did not want to lose but felt diminishing. So I began praying to understand what the Lord would suggest I do. Specific promptings came relative to changes I should make in my approach to daily study. The Spirit also suggested a focus of study and writing, still very much centered on Christ, that I was to pursue. As a result of obedience to those promptings, the subsequent months have been spiritually rewarding.

Just as the Spirit has been teaching and encouraging me, perhaps you have been feeling certain nudges as well. Maybe you, after reading this book, have also been asking yourself, "Now what? How will I sustain and build upon what I have just experienced?" Extra effort, adjustments, and improvements to past practices and habits may be necessary. I invite you to respond to spiritual impressions, as they will lead you to the Savior and allow you to feel deeply of His warmth, goodness, and love. I also invite you to consider making the reading of this book an annual tradition between Palm Sunday and Easter Sunday.

May careful and thoughtful reflection on the events that occurred from the first Palm Sunday to the first Easter Sunday further soften and prepare our hearts, strengthen our resolve to become more like the Savior, and prepare our spirits for that

From Palm Sunday to Easter Sunday

glorious day when He returns in majesty and power to reign rightfully as "King of kings, and Lord of lords" (1 Timothy 6:15). As you contemplate that glorious, eagerly hoped-for and not-distant day, ponder the words of the anthem, that powerful hymn, "Come, O Thou King of Kings."

> Come, O thou King of Kings!
> We've waited long for thee,
> With healing in thy wings,
> To set thy people free.
> Come, thou desire of nations, come;
> Let Israel now be gathered home.
>
> Come, make an end to sin,
> And cleanse the earth by fire,
> And righteousness bring in,
> That Saints may tune the lyre
> With songs of joy, a happier strain,
> To welcome in thy peaceful reign.
>
> Hosannas now shall sound
> From all the ransomed throng,
> And glory echo round
> A new triumphal song;
> The wide expanse of heaven fill
> With anthems sweet from Zion's hill.
>
> Hail! Prince of life and peace!
> Thrice welcome to thy throne!
> While all the chosen race

Their Lord and Savior own,
The heathen nations bow the knee,
And ev'ry tongue sounds praise to thee.[78]

---

[78] "Come, O Thou King of Kings," *Hymns*, no. 59.

Bibliography

Ballard, Melvin J. *Melvin J. Ballard: Crusader for Righteousness*. Salt Lake City: Bookcraft, 1966.

Benson, Ezra Taft. "Cleansing the Inner Vessel." *Ensign*. May 1986.

Benvegar, Charles Franklin. "The Wreckers." in *The Songs of the Free State Bards*. New World Books, 1967.

Callister, Tad R. *The Infinite Atonement*. Salt Lake City: Deseret Book, 2000.

Christofferson, D. Todd. "The Voice of Warning." *Ensign* or *Liahona*. May 2017.

Hinckley, Bryant S. *Sermons and Missionary Services of Melvin Joseph Ballard*. Salt Lake City: Deseret Book Company, 1949.

Holland, Jeffrey R. "None Were with Him." *Ensign* or *Liahona*. May 2009.

Huntsman, Eric D. *God So Loved the World*. Salt Lake City: Deseret Book, 2011.

Lewis, C. S. *Mere Christianity*, in *The Complete C. S. Lewis Signature Classics*, 1–178. New York City: HarperCollins, 2002.

Marsh, W. Jeffrey. *His Final Hours*. Salt Lake City: Deseret Book, 2000.

Maxwell, Neal A. "Jesus of Nazareth, Savior and King." *Ensign* or *Liahona*. May 1976.

McConkie, Bruce R. *Doctrinal New Testament Commentary*. Salt Lake City: Bookcraft, Inc., 1976.

———. *The Mortal Messiah: From Bethlehem to Calvary*, vol. 1. Salt Lake City: Deseret Book Company, 1979.

———. *The Mortal Messiah: From Bethlehem to Calvary*, vol. 3. Salt Lake City: Deseret Book Company, 1980.

———. "The Purifying Power of Gethsemane." *Ensign* or *Liahona*. May 1985.

Nelson, Russell M. "The Creation." *Ensign*. May 2000.

———. "Sacrament Meeting." *Ensign* or *Liahona*. August 2004.

Oaks, Dallin H. "Good, Better, Best." *Ensign* or *Liahona*. November 2007.

Penrose, Charles W. "The Second Advent." in *Doctrines of the Gospel Student Manual*. Salt Lake City: The Church of Jesus Christ of Latter-day Saints, 2000.

Smith, Joseph, Jr. "Discourse, between circa 26 June and circa 2 July 1839, as Reported by Willard Richards." *The Joseph Smith Papers* 17, October 5, 2018. http://www.josephsmithpapers.org/paper-summary/discourse-between-circa-26-june-and-circa-2-july-1839-as-reported-by-willard-richards/3.

Talmage, James E. *Jesus the Christ*. Salt Lake City: Deseret Book Company, 1982.

The Life and Teachings of Jesus and His Apostles, 2nd ed. Salt Lake City: The Church of Jesus Christ of Latter-day Saints, 1978.

Uchtdorf, Dieter F. "Pride and the Priesthood." *Ensign* or *Liahona*. November 2010.

———. "The Way of the Disciple." *Ensign* or *Liahona*. May 2009.

Widtsoe, John A. "Temple Worship." in *The Utah Genealogical and Historical Magazine*. vol. 12, ed. Nephi Anderson. Salt Lake City: The Deseret News Press, 1921.

About the Author

STEPHEN R. CHRISTIANSEN RECEIVED HIS B.A. from the University of Utah and his M.B.A. from Northwestern University. The following twenty years were spent with his growing family as he worked professionally in various locations in the U.S. and Latin America, including as Managing Director of Kimberly-Clark Corporation's businesses in Brazil, Peru, Ecuador, and Bolivia. Currently he works in the Office of the Presiding Bishopric, helping to lead a global organization design project. He has served in a variety of Church callings, including as a full-time missionary in Brazil, bishop, high councilor, and stake president. He is married to Suzanne Pool Christiansen. Together they have been blessed with four children and four grandchildren (and another on the way!).